Literary Criticism and Cultural Theory

Outstanding Dissertations

Edited by
William E. Cain
Wellesley College

A Routledge Series

LITERARY CRITICISM AND CULTURAL THEORY
WILLIAM E. CAIN, *General Editor*

A COINCIDENCE OF WANTS
The Novel and Neoclassical Economics
Charles Lewis

MODERN PRIMITIVES
Race and Language in Gertrude Stein, Ernest Hemingway, and Zora Neale Hurston
Susanna Pavloska

PLAIN AND UGLY JANES
The Rise of the Ugly Woman in Contemporary American Fiction
Charlotte M. Wright

DISSENTING FICTIONS
Identity and Resistance in the Contemporary American Novel
Cathy Moses

PERFORMING LA MESTIZA
Textual Representations of Lesbians of Color and the Negotiation of Identities
Ellen M. Gil-Gomez

FROM GOOD MA TO WELFARE QUEEN
A Genealogy of the Poor Woman in American Literature, Photography and Culture
Vivyan C. Adair

ARTFUL ITINERARIES
European Art and American Careers in High Culture, 1865–1920
Paul Fisher

POSTMODERN TALES OF SLAVERY IN THE AMERICAS FROM ALEJO CARPENTER TO CHARLES JOHNSON
Timothy J. Cox

EMBODYING BEAUTY
Twentieth-Century American Women's Writers' Aesthetics
Malin Pereira

MAKING HOMES IN THE WEST/INDIES
Constructions of Subjectivity in the Writings of Michelle Cliff and Jamaica Kincaid
Antonia MacDonald-Smythe

POSTCOLONIAL MASQUERADES
Culture and Politics in Literature, Film, Video, and Photography
Niti Sampat Patel

DIALECTIC OF SELF AND STORY
Reading and Storytelling in Contemporary American Fiction
Robert Durante

ALLEGORIES OF VIOLENCE
Tracing the Writing of War in Late
Twentieth-Century Fiction

Lidia Yuknavitch

NEW YORK AND LONDON

Published in 2001 by
Routledge
711 Third Avenue, New York, NY 10017
2 Park Square, Milton Park, Abingdon, Oxfordshire OX14 4RN

Routledge is an imprint of the Taylor & Francis Group

First issued in paperback 2013

Copyright © 2001 by Lidia Yuknavitch

All rights reserved. No part of this book may be reprinted or reproduced or utilized in any form or by any electronic, mechanical, or other means, now known or hereafter invented, including photocopying and recording, or in any information storage or retrieval system, without permission in writing from the publisher.

10 9 8 7 6 5 4 3 2 1

Library of Congress Cataloging-in-Publication Data
Yuknavitch, Lidia.
  Allegories of violence : tracing the writing of war in late twentieth-century fiction / Lidia Yuknavitch.
   p. cm. — (Literary criticism and cultural theory : the interaction of text and society)
  Includes bibliographical references and index.
  ISBN 0-415-93637-3 (alk. paper)
  1. American fiction—20th century—History and criticism. 2. War stories, American—History and criticism. 3. War stories, English—History and criticism. 4. Acker, Kathy, 1948- Empire of the senseless. 5. Silko, Leslie, 1948- Almanac of the dead. 6. Lessing, Doris May, 1919- Shikasta. 7. Heinemann, Larry. Paco's story. 8. DeLillo, Don. White noise. 9. Violence in literature. 10. Allegory.
I. Title. II. Literary criticism and cultural theory.
PS374.W35 Y85 2001
813'.509358—dc21   2001016010

ISBN13: 978-0-415-93637-8 (hbk)
ISBN13: 978-0-415-86678-1 (pbk)

Contents

Preface: War, the Serial — vii

Chapter I.
Introduction: War, History and Narrative — 3

Chapter II.
Vietnam and Narrative Reflexivity — 11

Chapter III.
War as Narrative Discourse — 35

Chapter IV.
Nuclear Ideology and Narrative Displacement — 55

Chapter V.
War, Sexuality, and Narrative — 75

Chapter VI.
Narrative Fragmentation: Toward an American Resistance Literature — 97

Chapter VII.
Conclusion: The Writing of War — 121

Bibliography — 127

Index — 133

PREFACE
War, The Serial

1. A cloud blooms up from a funnel to a mushroom, filling the frame, unmistakable in its imagery; a city's name burns into consciousness.
2. American soldiers half standing, half leaning from the ground up to erect an American flag; later a statue of the same gesture.
3. A girl running, screaming toward the camera's eye; she is on fire. The word "Napalm." The words "Viet Cong."
4. A desert field of fire, economy at war with fundamentalism; an award winning documentary.

LIKE MOST AMERICANS BORN IN THE 1960s OR LATER, MY EXPERIENCE OF WAR IS almost exclusively representational. I know war because photographs, books, television, and movies have represented it for me. I know World War because I know *Dr. Strangelove* (1964), *Slaughterhouse Five*, (1969), and *All Quiet on the Western Front* (1929). I know World War II from images of a swastika and a man with a mustache, his hand jutting forth and up, from *The Diary of Anne Frank* (1947), and from a whole host of Holocaust literature. In fact, "Holocaust Studies" was born in my generation, and I have at this point taught courses on "The Novels of War." I know old wars from new representations such as *Saving Private Ryan* (1998). I know Vietnam because I was born the year Kennedy was shot, because of a fascination I developed with the Zapruder footage of his death, because I saw the film *The Deer Hunter* (1978) at age fifteen and couldn't eat for a week, because I saw the film *Apocalypse Now* (1979) at age sixteen and became obsessed with film, art, and literature. I know Vietnam because Tim O'Brien, Larry Heinemann, and Michael Herr wrote it for me. It may even be true, at this point, that I know The Gulf War because of the television production "Desert Storm," the leftist counter-culture critiques from writers such as Noam Chomsky, Norman Schwartzkopf's statements about the bombs bursting in air looking "just like Christmas," the award winning documentary featuring endless imagery of burning oil, and perhaps even the recent film, *Three Kings* (1999), where I was particularly taken with the twists in the story as well as the editing, splicing, and cinematography; less so with the politics.

I know the male soldier's story because it is axiomatic for what we mean when we say war.

Other books and movies come to mind: *The Red Badge of Courage* (1895), *Parade's End* (1924-28), *A Farewell to Arms* (1929), *The Green Berets* (1968), *Patton* (1970), *Gravity's Rainbow* (1973), *Dispatches* (1978), *Close Quarters* (1979), *The Killing Fields* (1984), *Full Metal Jacket* (1987), *Born On The Fourth of July* (1989), *The Things They Carried* (1990), *Schindler's List* (1993), and *The Thin Red Line* (1998). Half of the books on this list have also been made into movies, some more than once. Half the movies have inspired more books and other movies. In addition, if you type in "Fields of Fire," "The Green Berets," or "War and Peace" on an Internet search engine today, some of the first sites you'll find are video games and sites carrying the names of those older representations.

Stop me when this sounds familiar.

My point is not to trivialize or diminish the horror and seriousness of war, nor de-valorize the soldier's story. I am simply pointing to a phenomenon which I believe is common in American experience since Vietnam. If we—and by "we" I mean a quite self conscious construction of American civilian society born after 1960 as well as a "we" predicated on the dominant culture's representations—exclude the participants, who, by the way, grow fewer and fewer as military technology advances, and if we exclude the primary victims, it is true, or true enough, that our understanding of war is fundamentally arrived at by and through representation. The television report. The linguistic catch-phrases: "surgical strike," "SMART Missile," "Trench Warfare," "Guerrilla Warfare." The bestselling novel. The award winning feature film. A novelist's passion. A director's vision.

More specifically, as World War has faded out of the picture (out of the *events* picture, but certainly not out of motion pictures, yes?), other kinds of wars have replaced it. Let me give an example. As writers such as James William Gibson have so astutely pointed out, our post-Vietnam understanding of war has some distinguishing characteristics. We might begin by saying that we have a kind of traditional war culture understanding in this country. In that story we base our understanding on the experiences of the white soldier male, his heroisms, his victimizations, his battles, wounds, and braveries. Like the traditional war culture that this country understands, the post-Vietnam culture reflects stories of the white soldier male. According to Gibson in *Warrior Dreams: Violence and Manhood In Post-Vietnam America*, two stories in particular emerge: that of the white soldier male as hero, and that of the white soldier male as victim (usually "restored" to heroic status). Traditionally, one story valorizes the lone gunman who acts independently

Preface

and heroically, and the other reflects the good soldier who is a member of an authorized military body and defends national honor in heroic ways. As Gibson argues, "these mythologies, sometimes overlapping, sometimes competing, have at different times defined the martial mentality of the country" (17). One need only make a mental catalogue of their knowledge of the war novels and films of the last 30 years in order to test this theory.

Those stories began to take on serious representational weight around 1941, when, as many have documented, war-related movies began to saturate cinema. By 1948 the war movie as a convention, like the novel of war, had multiplied the events to cinematic proportions. Again, according to Gibson between 1948 and 1968 "approximately 1,200 war movies were made" (22). Like filmmakers, novelists, journalists, photojournalists, editors and publishers, broadcast and print reporters and news agencies, politicians, governmental agencies, and religious figureheads have all contributed *representational material* to what we think of as the story of war in American culture. But the story is not—nor has it ever been—stable. For Gibson, a "New War" has been created sometime during the 1970s and 1980s, one that is distinct from earlier versions of American War culture. For Gibson, the "New War," at least in representational terms, has four distinguishing characteristics: 1) it is fought primarily by paramilitary warriors; 2) the new battles are fought with a violence less tethered to moral character and more connected to shock and a hunger for killing; 3) the "New War appears to be a war without end" (30); and 4) the "New War has nothing at all to say about what kind of society will be created after the enemy is vanquished" (31). This is the site where my discussion enters the picture, and in particular, I am interested in novelistic discourse as one of many forms that has contributed to the representational material that has created our contemporary understanding of this "New War." This is also the site where my discussion deviates from others, including Gibson's, in that I am not analyzing the soldier, masculinity, the activity of battles and killing, or the realm of the battlefield and the development of military technology. I mean instead to discuss how writing and reading are part of the production of the "New War" story.

It seems at the very least fair to state that, if war is for the most part a matter of representation for the majority of people in America, then its meaning is for the most part a matter of interpretation. For traditionally we have understood representation not as the thing itself, but something that stands in for it. Thus it remains endlessly open to different points of view. What the background or education of the reader/viewer is, what their political bent is, how much or little they trust television or media, how seriously they take film as a mode of production that can tell us something about ourselves, whether or not they read novels, how they read novels (as pure entertainment, psychoanalytically, historically, deconstructively)—all these angles and more determine how we will read war. This includes rereadings of past wars, conflicting readings of present wars, and speculations about future wars.

Preface: War, The Serial

My study attempts to carve out a small corner of conversation at the site of war's *discursive* representation. It is at least possible that how war is written in late twentieth century texts can show us something about our place in and out of it. The ideological territories I would like to illuminate are those ordinarily repressed by the soldier's story: the possible changing telos or goal of war, the narrative manifestation of war in ordinary human lives, the relationship between war and gender, redefinitions of war from the point of view of Native peoples.

Representationally, I am raising slightly different questions. In the "New War," do we get new Icons, or an entirely different kind of representation? Is social order restored or left in ruins? It is possible that the writing of war can show us something about shifting definitions of violence, identity, and social existence, if we let go for a moment of our sacred imagery—the soldier male, the mushroom cloud, the soldier's pushing up the flag against evil, the little girl on fire running for her life, the slick black economic field of fire—long enough to read what's underneath.

ALLEGORIES OF VIOLENCE

CHAPTER I
Introduction: War, History and Narrative

> All along the Somme, our fathers and grandfathers tasted the first terrors of the twentieth century. In the Somme Valley the back of language broke. It could no longer carry its former meanings. World War I changed the life of words and images in art, radically and forever. It brought our culture into industrialized death.
>
> —Robert Hughes, *The Shock of the New*

AT THE HEART OF THIS STUDY IS THE IDEA THAT WE HAVE BEEN LIVING IN THE AGE OF mass-produced, industrialized death that Robert Hughes speaks of for almost a century, and that our words and images tell the story of a war that pervades an epoch. The breakdown in meaning that Hughes identified as a result of the crisis of World War I has given way to a continual breakdown in meaning characteristic of the social order of the late twentieth-century and early twenty-first-century. More specifically, marxist, poststructuralist, deconstructionist, and psychoanalytic discourses have each contributed to a new articulation of social organization in late twentieth-century life. I am speaking here of the ways in which theoretical, philosophical, historical and political discourses since World War II have contributed to the articulation of a modern understanding of history, identity and social organization. New definitions have emerged based on the idea that history, identity and language are unstable, including but not limited to the work of Freud, Lacan, Jameson, Adorno, Barthes, Derrida, Foucault, Baudrillard, Deleuze and Guattari. Terms generated from such discourses give the late twentieth-century several names: postmodern, multinationalist, post-industrial, consumer society. One thing is lacking in these possible definitions if we reflect back on Hughes' statement. There is no World War that might help to define our struggles, or help to articulate our period. In its place we have something closer to serial-

3

ized war, though we still continue to name wars individually, particularly in relation to television reporting ("Desert Storm" and "The Gulf War"). How then do we read the broken back of language in such an age? And, more specific to my study, is there such a thing as a war novel?

At first glance the novels I have grouped together for this study may appear to have little to do with one another. Only one of them self-consciously addresses a war with which we are familiar, Vietnam. One of them is a science fiction novel, two have been identified by literary critics as postmodern, and one has resisted categorization altogether. Each of the novels I have chosen approaches the relation of war, history and representation in a slightly different way. For instance, if I were to ask how the novels in my study define "war," it would seem that each would provide a different answer. *Paco's Story*, the Vietnam novel by Larry Heinemann, defines war as something that is factually and experientially lost, available only in glimpses and conflicting representations. Doris Lessing's novel, *Shikasta*, tells the story of war as a structure of consciousness from the point of view of extraterrestrial beings. Still another version is Don DeLillo's novel, *White Noise*, in which war as we knew it within history has been commodified and strewn out randomly across consumer culture. Kathy Acker's novel *Empire of the Senseless* stages several versions of patriarchy and constructions of sexuality as war. Lastly, Leslie Marmon Silko's massive historical novel, *Almanac of the Dead*, reduces all definitions of war to issues of economy. Thus, any definition of war or of the contemporary war novel would have to be provisional and transitory. It is as if war as a theme has been dislocated from history and scattered across narrative. What is still true is that the genre of the novel, the concept of history, and the fact of war still exist; we still make fictions of ourselves even if those fictions are unstable, we still understand ourselves as inhabiting a history even if that history is unstable, and we certainly still wage war, even if the definitions of war are changing.

One angle from which to approach the questions of this study is to look at the art of this century in general and its relation to war. In his comprehensive and illuminating study of modern art and history, *The Shock of The New: The Hundred Year History of Modern Art—Its Rise, Its Dazzling Achievement, Its Fall*, Robert Hughes argues for an inextricable link between art and social, politcal and economic order. According to Hughes, one may trace the history of technological advance by and through artistic production, and vice versa. In particular he traces the influence of technological advance as a kind of "pressure" on art. For instance, the machine age characterized by the movement from steam to electricity and including such discoveries as the cinematograph and the gramophone disc (1894), X-Rays (1895), movie cameras (1895), the first powered flight (1903), the theory of relativity (1905) and the nuclear age, brought with it the excitement of the "benevolent" machine, reflected in artists such as Marcel Duchamp, Robert Dulaunay, and many Cubists, including Pablo Picasso (14-15). In contrast, by 1945 the myth of a "good technology" had eroded as events and symbols such as Hiroshima and the phenomenon of Nazi Germany came to exemplify the new technological zeitgeist of the century. By the end of World War II, television and photography changed the relation between art and history forever. As Hughes notes, in 1937 when Picasso painted *Guernica*, the phenomenon of television broadcasting was only a year old. According to Hughes, *Guernica* marks the last great history painting and the last great political statement about war in art (110–111). It may be that the last great historical novel of war, like the last World War, happened sometime between 1914 and 1945.

While it is certainly true that the war novel after 1914 began to shift its forms and techniques in relation to changes in social life and economy, as I will discuss, the post-1960 war novel has turned from telling the story of the event of war to telling the story of language itself, trading the value of the event for the efficacy of representation. In other words, as the fronts and technique of war have shifted, the content and form of the novel have as well. The novels I have chosen re-introduce war into discussions concerning changes in our social life and their relation to representation.

However, the available critical frames for a discussion of novels of war after 1960 are limited to a certain version of the link between war and literature. The role of the novel in the articulation of war has been charted by Arne Axelsson in *Restrained Response: American Novels of the Cold War;* Tobin Siebers' *Cold War Criticism and the Politics of Skepticism;* and Thomas Schab's *American Fiction in the Cold War*, among other books. In particular, as Paul Fussell charts in his literary history, *The Great War and Modern Memory*, war is a major source of our literary history, and conversely, the forms of literary history inform our accounts of war, as if literary history were the only way to talk about war. In 1928, as Fussell notes, a literary outpouring of World War I literature produced Aldous Huxley's *Point Counterpoint*, Erich Maria Remarque's *All Quite on the Western Front*, Siegfried Sasson's *Memoirs of a Fox hunting Man*, Max Plowman's *Subaltern on the Somme*, and Evelyn Waugh's *Decline and Fall*, among others. In each case Fussell shows how the authors not only tell stories about war, but locate war through necessarily literary forms, particularly irony, romance, and satire, forms that were already available in literary history prior to World War I (myth, romance, and irony, for instance, exemplified in the course of ancient literature from scriptures to Roman comedy, medieval through Renaissance to realist to modern). One might say that literary history shaped our understanding of contemporary war before it ever happened.

Fussell goes on to argue that in the years during and after the Second World War, after "heaping of violence upon violence," the war novel reached its fullest and starkest form of irony. This idea intersects my own study, since my discussion contrasts the form of World War I novels and modernist war novels to the war novels written after 1960 in an effort to record narrative similarities and differences, beginning with the irony that Fussell identifies.[1] The narrative language of the period after World War II constructs a different response to war than does the narrative language before it. Specifically, unlike a tradition of war novels that came out of the Great War, which located war on the battlefield, the texts in my study critique the relation between war and representation. In particular, formal changes in the novel of war after 1960 must be charted and historicized. Whereas war has been a periodizing feature for charting literarary history, I would like to argue that representation now maps out or historicizes conflict.

The genres of the realist and modernist novels can also tell us something about the relation between war and representation and the critical limits of discussion. As traced in Robert Scholes and Robert Kellog's *The Nature of Narrative*, Wayne Booth's *The Rhetoric of Fiction*, and Northrup Frye's *Anatomy of Criticism*, the realist novel emerged at a critical juncture in European history in which the understanding of the relationship between history and representation was changing. In general realism has been understood as a periodizing concept that identifies a nineteenth-century movement and as an identifying mode of representation in which a claim is made that art reflects ordinary life. Whether or not that reflection is stable or unstable has been an issue of debate since Plato. Traditionally, realist conventions were understood as neutral descriptions of reality, characteristic of the works of Balzac, Dickens, and Flaubert. More recently, poststructuralist critics have theorized that literary representations are constituted by arbitrary conventions; thus no valid ground for a truly realist discourse exists. The realist war novel had a very specific definition and aim. It depended heavily on mimetic description because it tried to depict the living conditions, the daily experience, the equipment and weaponry, and the landscape of men at the front, such as in Émile Zola's *La Débâcle*, or Tolstoy's *War and Peace*, and including many twentieth-century works such as Norman Mailer's *The Naked and the Dead* or Ford Maddox Ford's *Parade's End*. The primary goal of the war novel was to educate the reader about the truth of war. Although not every realist war novel employed a mimetic or reflection theory of language, most narrative techniques were intended to create the strongest illusion of reality possible, as Evelyn Cobley argues in "Description in Realist Discourse."

Critics generally agree that World War I and World War II changed the form of the novel. In a way, World War served as a representational crisis in which a radical discontinuity between nineteenth-century versions of social order reflected by realism and newly emergent social orders reflected by very different forms arose. The disjunction between realism and modernism, for instance, was reproduced as a formal feature in novelistic narrative. The modernist novel marked a fundamental historical discontinuity from the forms of realism, including a sense of alienation, loss, and despair resulting in the search for inner meaning unavailable in the chaotic outside world, and a loss of stable authority in language (Huyssen, 188-190; Wallis, xiii). Vital ideas about language and meaning also changed. Modernist novels marked not only the end of a certain experience of history, they marked as well the end of certain models of representation, as writers such as Joyce, Faulkner and Woolf exemplify. Wartime writers in particular seemed to let go of the representational authority that characterized realism and concentrate instead on the novel's formal capacities to reflect how war challenges the very foundations of meaning and history. The debate over realist and modernist conventions and their relation to history has been well charted in contemporary criticism, from Erich Auerbach's *Mimesis: The Representation of Reality in Western Literature* (1953), to Ernst Gombrich's *Art and Illusion* (1960), to George Levine's *The Realistic Imagination* (1981) and so on. However, changes in the formal features of the war novel post 1960 have yet to be fully charted. The fact remains that the war novels written by modernist authors that I use as models of contrast in my study, including those of Graves, Woolf and Hemingway display a narrative language that is radically different than the novels in my study, leaving the question open as to how one might historicize their language.

It would seem that the model that best presents itself for charting this new narrative language would be the literary postmodern. After all, as Jameson argues, the formal features of the literary postmodern reflect changes in late twentieth-century life; one would assume that definition to include modern warfare. It is for this reason that much of my critical frame comes from Jameson's discussion of postmodernism. According to Jameson in "Postmodernism and Consumer Society," postmodernism is a periodizing concept which articulates the relation between new formal features in culture and the rise of a new kind of social life and economic order. Jameson identifies the 1960s in particular as a key period in which postmodernism's most important formal features emerge in architecture, art, music and literature. But what does the literary postmodern have to do with war? Though Jameson calls Vietnam the first terribly postmodern war, he never fully articulates why. Why not modern? Why not avant-garde? Citing Michael Herr's Vietnam war novel *Dispatches*, Jameson suggests that this particular war had particular effects tied to late capitalism:

> this first terrible postmodernist war cannot be told in any of the traditional pardigms of the war novel or movie—indeed that breakdown of all previous narrative paradigms is, along with the breakdown of any shared language through which the veteran might convey such experience, among the principle subjects of the book and may be said to open up the place of a whole new reflexivity. (*Postmodernism, or The Cultural Logic of Late Capitalism*, 45)

If World War broke the back of language, perhaps Vietnam left us with the question of what we would do with those broken forms. My study begins where Jameson leaves off, with a Vietnam war novel, in order to ask how war figures into discussions of the novel and how the novel fits into discussion about war. Postmodernism thus has a limited role in my discussion. The postmodern text articulates specific late capitalist and modern warfare developments differently than modernist texts did. However, realism, modernism and postmodernism all move forward and backward in history, because they can be understood as temporarily overlapping.

In charting the formal similarities and differences between these novels I hope to illuminate and historicize how the genre of the war novel has broken down and changed as a result of contemporary experiences of war. I have identified the following as dominant narrative strategies:

a. *narrative reflexivity:* the disruption of syntax or syntagmatic relations. The disruption of linear time and narrative sequentiality in favor of processes of repetition or accumulation.
b. *cross-use of discourses:* narrative attempts to "flatten" history or historic markers (dates, documents, figures). The displacement of metanarratives replaced by the cross-use of discourses from other disciplines, myths, parables, or other cultural texts.
c. *breakdown of narrative content:* archetypal themes are broken down and stripped of their prior narrative weight, reconfigured as a continual series of other texts, signs, images, and metanarratives. For example, the romance, the quest, and a Western metaphysical tradition represented in literature of war as agon.
d. *citation and pastiche:* the breakdown of the authority of the literary artifact. The use of prior textual and artistic material, the imitation of prior textual and artistic material, the inclusion of prior textual and artistic material in montage, citation, or appropriated forms.
e. *narrative fragmentation:* the breaking down of the subject, the disappearance of the hero, the division of the protagonist into parts. The division of the plot into non-chronological and even random pieces.

The first chapter, "Vietnam and Narrative Reflexivity," is a close reading of Larry Heinemann's Vietnam novel *Paco's Story*. In it I isolate a narrative strategy which forecloses modernist narrative options and replaces them with a new poetics of reflexivity characterized by the accumulation of images, syntactic doublings, and the dissolution of an autonomous and authoritative narrator. I argue that the novel *Paco's Story* breaks down the accessibility and authorizing function of facts and the position of the soldier as an authentic "author" of his experience. The narration moves onto a plane of indeterminacy, contingency, and repetition—a strategy I am calling narrative reflexivity. The soldier hero dissolves in his own telling as narrative means and the inability to deliver experience to a reader become the novel's focus.

The second chapter is a study of the cross-use of discourses in Doris Lessing's science fiction novel, *Shikasta*. The novel serves as an example of the changing definitions of war since World War II. In this first book of her *Canopus in Argos* series, Lessing writes the history of earth through the eyes of a superior species from another galaxy. Their viewpoint dissolves the "spe-

Introduction

cial status" given to wars such as Vietnam by Americans and instead situates it within a larger story of perpetual violence instigated not by Communists against a free world, but by the white races against all other races of the world. I argue that Lessing "flattens" history by condensing and listing in a series what are our most important historical events and dates in Britain and the United States. I go on to argue that the cross-use of discourses from science, private journals, myth, and governmental reports create a narrative that exposes how war is not located exclusively on a battlefield, but also in our structures of consciousness and our cultural productions. The "battlefields" in the novel emerge as social, sexual, domestic, and representational.

In chapter three I explore the variety of ways in which Don DeLillo's novel *White Noise* addresses the nuclear bomb as an idea that takes primacy over the event of nuclear war. I argue that the novel relates the atomization of the real and the primacy of representation to a nuclear legacy and a new kind of death which pervades contemporary culture. For example, the novel's three sections are titled "Waves and Radiation," "The Airborne Toxic Event," and "Dylarama,"—all metaphors for the nuclear—and Jack's family structure is a parody of the "nuclear" family. I identify how the narrative strategies in the novel center on the activity of learning how to read the signs of our contemporary times—television, cinema, and advertising—instead of historic events and artifacts. At this point in my discussion I bring in the literary postmodern as an aesthetic category and study its relation to modernism, because the main character in the novel, Jack Gladney, is a vehicle for contrasting the modernist aesthetic to the postmodernist, and because the narrative structures in the novel expose the limits of mimetic modernist forms.

In Kathy Acker's novel, *Empire of the Senseless,* the apocalypse, nuclear, economic, social, sexual, has already happened. Geographic and historic war zones have been replaced by psycho-sexual land mines. In order to achieve mobility at all, the main character, Abhor, must become fragmented and split—arguably formal features of the literary postmodern—in order to dislocate herself from the society's models of war, all sexual in nature. In this chapter I explore the breakdown of character into a fragmented and constantly changing subject. As a figure of the coding of war, Abhor inhabits a truly postmodern landscape where the "deserts of the real" are a "patriarchal wasteland." I identify deconstructive pastiche and appropriation as narrative reactions to a culture saturated by violence and war, and I open the question up as to whether or not these features begin to "fit" a list of postmodern literary forms.

In the last chapter I look at Leslie Marmon Silko's novel *Almanac of the Dead* as the logical next step in the trajectory of my inquiry. I come back to the possible definitions of history, the novel, and war, as well as the relation between them. I also depart from the literary postmodern as an aesthetic model by pointing to its limits as Silko's novel both engages and resists its forms. Like the representation of war in all the novels, war is perpetual in Silko's novel, but different in that one people resist the movements of another over all of American history. *Almanac of the Dead* takes capitalism and America as a Super Power to its logical conclusion, the control of minority races for the use of white economic development. Through a process of radical narrative fragmentation which structures the novel, historic record gives way to an almanac of ghosts, corpses, and oral traditions mixed-up with contemporary forms of communication and destruction. In this chapter I explore how narrative fragmentation works to split open the dominant history of America with an American resistance literature.

These novels profoundly demilitarize our understandings of war. In other words, by subordinating the traditional content of war—the soldier at the front or the historical event— to formal features such as narrative reflexivity, the cross-use of discourse, narrative displacement, pastiche and fragmentation in the story of war, each novel challenges us to ask what would happen if we understood war as discursive. Close attention to the formal features of the texts in this study produces a new, provisional reading practice in which war works textually. Instead of reading war as an issue of content, the novels in my study suggest that we read war as a trope, a figure of thought on which meaning turns. The writing of war, the troping of war happens at the level of narrative language, as I will show.

In *Pure War* Sylvere Lotringer remarks that war is everywhere, but we no longer have the means of recognizing it. My study attempts to build new forms of reading that might help us to recognize the changing forms of war, even if we do not want to hear any more about it, even if we are saturated with it, even if it pervades an epoch.

NOTES

1. I am limiting my comparisons to First World War novels and not Second World War novels because the literature of the Second World War, as Evelyn Colbey argues in "Narrating the Facts of War" only rarely aimed to render descriptive accounts of life at the front. She correctly notes that press and film coverage performed many of the services the First World War novelist considered to be his project.

CHAPTER II
Vietnam and Narrative Reflexivity

WRITING ABOUT WAR, T. S. ELIOT REMARKED THAT "IN THE FACE OF . . . WAR WE must measure the suffering, direct and indirect, against the spiritual goods which may come of suffering" (*Selected Prose* 209). Eliot emphasized the importance of morality in matters of war by suggesting that suffering has a spiritual justification. In his collection of war stories, Tim O'Brien problematizes the relationship between truth and morality: "A true war story is never moral. It does not instruct nor encourage virtue, nor suggest models of proper human behavior, nor restrain men from doing the things they have always done. If a story seems moral, do not believe it" (*The Things They Carried* 76–77). Of course, O'Brien is referring to modes of storytelling specific to the Vietnam war. As Vietnam authors like O'Brien, Michael Herr, Larry Heinemann and John McAfee, among others, have shown us, the truth of the war story post 1960 may not be pretty: "As a first rule of thumb, therefore, you can tell a true war story by its absolute and uncompromising allegiance to obscenity and evil" (*The Things They Carried* 70). Morality, it would seem, has somehow lost its narrative place.

Like O'Brien, Larry Heinemann represents the Vietnam war as a story that wrecks its own telling. In his first novel, *Close Quarters*, Heinemann showed us a narration deeply troubled by the main character's inability to piece together a story without an almost torturous personal sacrifice. *Paco's Story*, Heinemann's second novel and the subject of this chapter, is not a war story at all; the narrator challenges the reader with this information: "Let's begin with the first clean fact, James: This aint no war story" (3). It is as if something is wrong with the war story, at least from the narrator's point of view. From the first line the reader must wonder, why isn't it a war story, if it isn't one then what is it, and what is the problem with war stories? To which Heinemann offers:

11

War stories are out—one, two, three, and a heave-ho, into the lake you go with all the other alewife scuz and foamy harbor scum. But isn't it a pity. All those crinkly, soggy sorts of laid-by tellings crowded together as thick and pitiful as street cobbles, floating mushy bellies up, like so much moldy shag rug (dead rusty-ass doornails and smelling so peculiar and un-Christian). (3)

If these are the "first clean facts" about a war story, then both facts and war stories are curiously unstable, deeply suspicious, and relegated to the realm of harbor scum, scuz, soggy mush and moldy inanimate corpses floating belly side up. In other words, war stories are floating refuse and debris. What readers are confronted with is and is not a war story. The content of the novel, war, is dissolving. In its place we find *Paco's Story*.

In that dissolving I would like to trace how the formal features of *Paco's Story* interrupt any chance at traditional narrative development. When I say dissolving I mean the loss of clarity or definition of character or narrative shape. In place of narrative development we are given narrative reflexivity, a kind of turning back on itself. The specific forms of narrative reflexivity that surface in the novel begin to show us how the theme of war gives way to questions of representation. In particular, the novel's two most important thematic events, the wounding of Paco Sullivan at a terrible firefight turned massacre at Fire Base Harriette, and the rape of a sniper girl during the war, are condensed into formal questions, as I will argue. My argument in this chapter is twofold: in the first part of my discussion, I plan to trace the narrative strategies featured in Heinemann's novel and discuss how they interrupt or arrest narrative development. In particular I will look at the unstable position of the narrator, a reflexivity emerging from passages that repeat words or that produce an accumulation of images, and what I am calling syntactic doublings. These narrative strategies are the basis for Heinemann's distinctive poetics. In the second part of my discussion I will look at how those narrative strategies find their strongest and most specific form in the figure of the dissolving male body.

Critical responses to *Paco's Story* since its publication in 1986 vary. Some tend to focus on the ethical issues surrounding not only the Vietnam war, but also the novel's two central violent events, the wounding of Paco and the gruesome gang-rape of a Vietnamese sniper girl. Feminist readings in particular, such as Susan Jefford's *The Remasculinization of America*, locate the theme of the novel at the level of male violence and its relationship to constructions of gender. Other critics tend to study the distanced narration and the multiple-voiced structure of the novel as formal strategies unique to Vietnam war novels, such as Gregory L. Morris in "Reading War Stories: Larry Heinemann's *Paco's Story* and the Serio-Comic Tradition." The novel receives brief notice in Thomas Myer's *Walking Point: American Narratives of Vietnam*, and in his essay "Dispatches from Ghost Country: The Vietnam War in Recent American Fiction." Perhaps most common are the works that suggest

Vietnam and Narrative Reflexivity

that the Vietnam war is continually being re-invented: Philip Beidler's book *Re-writing America: Vietnam Authors in Their Generation*; *Inventing Vietnam: The War in Film and Television*, edited by Michael Anderegg; Vince Gotera's book, *Radical Visions: Poetry by Vietnam Veterans*; *Tell Me Lies About Vietnam: Cultural Battles for the Meaning of War*, edited by Alf Louvre and J. Walsh; and *The Legacy: The Vietnam War in the American Imagination*, edited by Michael Shafer. What most critics seem to agree on is that war literature after Vietnam tells a very different kind of story than the war literature that preceded it.

Before we can talk about representations of the Vietnam war it helps to talk about the war stories that came before it. Critical responses to First World War literature can tell us a great deal about past understandings of the relationship between experience and representation that appears in the First World War novel. For example, like literature in general, the war literature of this century up to Vietnam has been characterized by many critics as mimetic in nature. In particular, First World War novels displayed toward their thematic contents a mimetic relationship between history and representation. The actuality of war was imitated in the art, following a broader mimentic tradition outlined by writers such as Eric Auerbach. For instance, Peter G. Jones argues in *War and the Novel*, that the novel quite literally mirrors historical reality.

Similarly, in what is widely regarded by historians and literary critics who study war novels as a rather definitive text by Paul Fussell, *The Great War and Modern Memory*, an emphasis is given to the *literary* nature of historical events. In addition, in his 1989 book on World War II, *Wartime: Understanding and Behavior in the Second World War*, Fussell continues to assert that a literary history of war is our most powerful record of the experience. According to Fussell in *The Great War and Modern Memory*, war is a "historical experience with conspicuous imaginative and artistic meaning," wherein "the literary dimensions of the trench experience itself" reveal themselves (x). For instance, Fussell finds archetypal literary forms of romance, irony and heroism inside letters, poems and stories meant to document the experience of World War.[1] Paradigm cases for this notion would be Robert Graves and Ernest Hemingway, who each wrote war novels in 1929, *Goodbye to All That* and *A Farewell to Arms* respectively.[2] In 1928 several novels of World War I emerged with the same kinds of literary forms directing the representation of the war experience, particularly Erich Maria Remarque's *All Quiet on the Western Front*, Siegried Sassoon's *Memoirs of a Foxhunting Man*, Max Plowman's *Subaltern on the Somme*, among others.

I intend to use Fussel's claims as a platform for my study because his book is a literary history of war. In particular Fussell studies the memoir, poetry, and the novel as forms that accurately reflect the experience of war; furthermore, Fussell claims that representation is the only way we can remember war once it has happened. Two limits to his study are his memorializing of the white, male soldier as victim and his successful canonization of literary works written exclusively by men. The story emerging from *The*

Great War and Modern Memory is that British and American soldiers are the tragic victims of war. The stability of this story depends on the idea that war happens to no one but British and American soldiers. The novels in my study undercut that notion by designing worlds of war that infect the entire fabric of social existence, including our structures of consciousness.

Fussell begins his study by looking at the narrators of war. He points out that the most important feature of First World War literature is above all the experience of memory, or, more precisely, how soldiers in particular recount the stories of their experience, through documentary, memoir, poetry, letters, and the novel. In dealing with the memory of war, participants and witnesses employ what Fussell terms "irony assisted recall":

> By applying to the past a paradigm of ironic action, a remembered is enabled to locate, draw forth, and finally shape into significance an event or a moment which otherwise would merge without meaning into the general undifferentiated stream. (30)

In other words, the war witness must distance himself or herself from the experience in order to register the chaos of war as a form with deeper moral or spiritual significance. The danger involved in relating the experience directly would be to produce a "general undifferentiated stream." More specifically, Fussell claims that The Great War, and the texts that try to describe it, stage a central theme: the proximity of violence to meaning, and the individual's attempt to "shape into significance" the experience of war. Literary history already contained the forms from which the war novel would be built—the romance, the quest, the figure of the soldier hero. In literary terms, he argues that the paradigm for the war memoir includes three elements common to the traditional literary romance: "first, a sinister or absurd or even farcical preparation; second, the unmanning experience of battle; and third, the retirement from the line to a contrasting (usually pastoral) scene, where there is time and quiet for consideration, meditation, and reconstruction" (130). These are the same kinds of narrative forms defined by Erich Auerbach in his influential book, *Mimesis: The Representation of Reality in Western Literature* when he analyses medieval romance of the twelfth and fifteenth centuries.

Thus, if we are to categorize novels according to Fussell's schema, a novel such as Hemingway's *A Farewell to Arms* is marked by several scenes that might serve as a paradigm for all First World War novels. In particular, descriptions of battles and memories of battles are interrupted by the narrator's retreat into pastoral scenes within which he can shape and perhaps transcend the overwhelming destruction of his experiences in war:

> That night in the hotel, in our room with the long empty hall outside and our shoes outside the door, a thick carpet on the floor of the room, outside the windows the rain falling and the room light and pleasant and cheerful,

Vietnam and Narrative Reflexivity 15

then the light out and it exciting with smooth sheets and the bed comfortable, feeling that we had come home, feeling no longer alone, waking in the night to find the other one there, and not gone away; all other things were unreal . . . If people bring so much courage to this world the world has to kill them to break them, so of course it kills them. (*A Farewell to Arms* 249)

Through such scenes of retreat from war into romance or meditation, Hemingway in effect reaches for a higher, moral ground upon which the wounds of war give way to moments we can more easily live with.

Or, in a very different example offered by Fussell, a text such as Graves' *Good-bye to All That*, which imposes the patterns of satire and farce onto the horrors of trench warfare, shows us something about the deep ironies generated by war. Instead of giving the "facts" of war characteristic of a documentary or autobiography, Graves often distills the facts of war into farce, as in his book *The Crowning Privilege*: "There is a funny-man in every barrack room (even if he is not really very funny)" (13). The distinction Fussell makes about novels from World War II shifts merely in degree. According to Fussell, novels such as Joseph Heller's *Catch-22*, *Closing Time* provide the same narrative patterns of irony and romance or satire. The difference is they are more stark or bare in their style.

The Vietnam novel is a specific example of how the form of the war novel has changed. If we examine the dominant narrative features of realist and modernist novels prior to 1960, for example, we might begin to chart important differences in contemporary representations. The realist novel displayed a language consistent with the ideas that truth could be arrived at through accurate, objective, narrative description, that historical events could be understood through allegories of progress and recorded through major literary traditions, archetypes and myths, and that symbolic meanings had a direct relationship to the experiences of individuals. An exemplary novelist would be Conrad. In terms of the literature of war, it is generally agreed upon by literary historians and critics that Thomas Hardy's collection of poems in 1914 reflects a direct medium for perceiving the events of war, Wilfred Owen exemplifies a poet who achieved the highest literary consciousness by telling the "truth" about war, Sigfried Sassoon represents a classic memoirist, and Robert Graves represents a classic satirist.

Like the modernist novel in general, the modernist war novel marked a fundamental historical discontinuity, a sense of alienation, loss and despair resulting in the search for inner meaning unavailable in the chaotic outside world (Huyssen 160–190; Jameson 1–67). Vital ideas about language and meaning also changed. First and Second World War novels marked not only the end of a certain experience of history, they marked as well the end of certain models of representation. They reflect a deep disturbance in language and meaning characteristic of the modernist novel in general and exemplified by the use of narrative strategies such as double entendres (prevalent for example in Joyce), the interruption of narrative with other devices of language such as ellipses, parenthesis, and syntactic fragmentation (exemplified in writers such as Faulkner, Stein and H.D.), and the juxtaposition of narrative against other major forms of "recording" life, such as journalism. It is important to note that modernist forms of mimesis were varied and in the process of dramatic change. For example, in the war texts of Virginia Woolf, and I am thinking particularly of *Jacob's Room*, *Three Guineas* and *Between The Acts* by Woolf as well as *Helen in Egypt* by H.D., new kinds of modernist mimesis were emerging. In Woolf, the reduction of narrative to brackets or the use of parentheses, for example, and in H.D., the use of reflexive grammar were self-conscious attempts to render war in the texture of a text.

For example, Virginia Woolf's use of narrative experimentation has been interpreted by some critics to reflect the move to represent external reality at the level of the texture of the novel. One can, for instance, easily find the impersonal filtering of factual reporting characteristic of journalism in *To The Lighthouse*: "[A shell exploded. Twenty or thirty young men were blown up in France, among them Andrew Ramsay, whose death, mercifully, was instantaneous.]" (152) Thus, locating war at the level of form was a practice first emerging in the modernist novel, and reflected changes in our understanding of language and representation. Language was set against itself, it challenged itself, and the stage was the novel. The mimetic theory of art was changing as well. Woolf's novels serve as an excellent transitional model between the First and Second World Wars and the wars and novels that followed. One might even say that Woolf is an example of a writer moving toward "the general undifferentiated stream" where events might merge without meaning into one another and into representation.

Whether or not we can call the contemporary war novel a radical break from modernist narrative strategies depends upon how we understand the historical and formal similarities and differences. One of the problems unique to war stories of Vietnam is the attempt to describe the nature of the experience because it keeps getting mixed up with its representation. As Philip D. Beidler describes in *American Literature and the Experience of Vietnam* (1982), the representation of Vietnam on television preceded the arrival home of its soldiers, leaving civilians and soldiers with a fundamental question about what happened. Beidler asks, "How, then, might one come up with some form of sensemaking for this thing—this experience already cast in the image of some insane metafiction recreating itself in actual life—and in the process find some reason to believe that the effort might be of some literary or cultural significance?" (10). In other words, soldiers returning from Vietnam were confronted with a set of images and representations that arrived before they did, a feature unique to both the Vietnam era and the history of mass media technology. Novelists such as Heinemann were confronted with the added problem of developing narrative strategies that might account for such advances in media communications that constructed headlines and television films that beat the story home. Unlike literature of the first and second World Wars, the literature of Vietnam emphasized a crisis between the witness of war and the reporter. The soldier's story was challenged by the more entertaining, even if violent, television program.

Vietnam caused novelists to hunt for a fictional mode that could accommodate that crisis. One place Larry Heinemann did not find an adequate fictional mode was inside the conventions of realism or modernism. Take for instance the main character in Hemingway's *A Farewell to Arms*. That novel did what all war novels of World War I did, in particular, it gave us a hero who fought for moral reasons, and who was wounded and challenged to recover those reasons. Similarly, films have produced heroic models that sustain a certain memory of war. For example, as James Gibson describes in his book *Warrior Dreams: Violence and Manhood in Post-Vietnam America*, pre-Vietnam movie and narrative representations gave us a set of soldiers whose "fighting ability flowed from moral strength" and whose anger and wounds were "just a way of keeping score." In other words, John Wayne, Gary Cooper, or Humphrey Bogart showed us something about virtuous men, not violent men, something about moral reasons to fight, not about killing and dismembering actual bodies, and something about the recovery of meaning following the chaos of war, not about the breakdown of meaning.

Vietnam, on the other hand, produced stories featuring bodies and reasons blown to bits. Furthermore, according to Gibson, "The scores of scenes featuring dismemberment, torture, and shredded bodies oozing fluids are absolutely central to the culture and are far removed from the older, dispassionate moral accounting" (30). John Wayne (*The Green Berets*, 1968) gives way to John Voight (*Coming Home*, 1978), Charlie Sheen (*Platoon*, 1986), and Tom Cruise (*Born on the Fourth of July*, 1989)—the war hero as we knew him began to dissolve. That older, dispassionate moral accounting is also absent in *Paco's Story*.

The most striking difference between Heinemann's novel and the war literature that precedes it is its form. The central narration is continually interrupted by other narrations, giving the novel a structure made up of fragments that do not quite "add up." By that I mean that all linear narrative impulses seem to be cut or interrupted by the presence of a never-ending supply of other narratives. In fact, the first "clean fact" isn't clean at all, if by clean the narrator means direct or clear. Whereas Hemingway's *A Farewell to Arms* showed us how reality was mirrored through representation in stable terms, *Paco's Story* empties the First World War novel of its structure and themes rather quickly, because it subordinates the theme or war and its possible symbolic value to the crisis of the act of remembering and representing. The main difference between war novels from the realist or modernist period and war novels post Vietnam is that the former claimed war could be represented, while the latter claim that war is unrepresentable, as I will argue. As the citation I used to open this discussion suggests, in Heinemann's novel, war as a theme is broken down and translated into a series of formal questions.

The first formal question that confronts the reader is the curious position of the narrator. Paco Sullivan is the single survivor of a firefight at Fire Base

Harriette. This ought to be the novel's central event. However, this event is challenged, or I would argue doubled, by another, the rape of a Vietnamese girl during the war. Paco is not the exclusive narrator. Rather, he inhabits the narration like a ghost, and the narration is made up of multiple narrative voices: other vets from other wars, Vietnam vets, random strangers, Paco's boss at the Texas Lunch, a girl in the town where Paco works after the war. Similarly, multiple narrative tones surface, from jovial to gruesome, from slang to poetic, as well as multiple images and story fragments.

The narration is not addressed directly to the reader, but rather to an equally ghost-like presence, an unexplained "James" to which the narration refers frequently. At times the narrator speaks to James in parentheticals, "(Pokorneyville, James, is a real place)" (4); "(for some piddling hand-to-mouth wage, James)" (4); "(whatever that is, James)" (5). At other times the narrator speaks to James directly. From the beginning Heinemann seems to abandon the possibility of the soldier's authority to tell the story of war by rendering the narrator's position to his own story in terms of reflexivity. In other words, unlike the narrator of First World War novels, *Paco's Story* shows us a narrator whose authority is distorted as it stretches across experience not to the reader, but to "James." So the narrator is not actually addressing the reader at all. A reader must ask what that interruption means, the interruption between witness and audience. In addition, the narrator's story is continually interrupted by other stories. Or, put slightly differently, unlike *A Farewell to Arms*, experience does not speak through representation but is "caught" between witness and audience, creating reflexivity where communication of experience used to be.

The formal reflexivity so central to this novel has its thematic versions too, for example, when the narrator problematizes the audience, an audience who has destroyed the war story even before it can be told:

> The people with the purse strings and apron strings gripped in their hot and soft little hands denounce war stories—with perfect diction and practiced gestures—as a geek-monster species of evil-ugly rumor (3).

But this thematic move is quickly transformed into a formal issue as well, and one must register the speed with which the theme dissolves into a formal issue. First the narrator is once distanced from the reader through the narrative construction of "James," and then the narrator projects even more distance between his account and the audience by jettisoning them away from himself as if they were characters too, characters who are more eager to see the "show" of Vietnam than to hear the depiction of the environment or actions of war. The reader is suddenly a formal question:

> Other people (getting witty and spry, floor-of-the-Senate, let-me-read- this-here-palaver-into-the-*Congressional-Record*, showboat oratorical) slipt one

Vietnam and Narrative Reflexivity

hand under a vest flap and slide one elegantly spit-shined wing-tip shoe forward ever so clever, and swear and be damned if all that snoring at war stories doesn't rattle windows for miles around. (4)

The more we read, the more we must locate our role as audience member from a list of disturbing possibilities.

Thus, Heinemann begins with the death of the war story, with the inability of the soldier to tell it and the inability of the audience to value it. In other words, the novel begins by projecting the world of the war novel itself, and then destabilizes that world, thus foregrounding the very process of its construction. The narrative mode displayed here begins a process whereby the war story will eventually be emptied of its thematic value.

By transforming the position of the reader into a formal question, Heinemann seems to want to emphasize irony, but not the ironic distance Fussell theorized. Rather, the narrative gives us the irony that our inability to understand the violence of war has been replaced by our desire to be entertained by violence. From the narrator's point of view, ironically, the only thing capable of getting this audience's attention is the presentation of images of violence: "Most folks will shell out hard-earned, greenback cash, every time, to see artfully performed, urgently fascinating, grisly and gruesome carnage" (4). Instead of the proximity of violence to meaning and the story of how individuals overcome that dangerous proximity, Heinemann gives us the conflation of violence *with* meaning, caused in part by the terrible gaps between experience, witness and audience. This is a formal strategy that subordinates the theme of war to the crisis in representation produced from trying to tell the story of war.

For example, even as the first chapter of the novel goes on and on about how little we care to hear about war stories, the violence central to the narrator's trauma is told in bald detail. Alpha company is massacred by friendly fire at Fire Base Harriet:

> We don't know what the rest of the company did, or the zips for that matter, but the 2nd squad of the 2nd platoon swapped that peculiar look around that travels from victim to victim in any disaster. We ciphered it out right then and there that we couldn't dig a hole deep enough, fast enough; couldn't crawl under something thick enough; couldn't drop our rifles, and whatnot, and turn tail and beat feet far enough but that this incoming wouldn't catch us by the scruff of the shirt, so to speak, and lay us lengthwise. (14-15)

It is important to focus here on the issue of form. Earlier I claimed that the breakdown of a particular war story paradigm reflected in the realist and modernist novels is part of the subject of the Vietnam novel. For the purposes of my present discussion, I would like to contrast that description with the following passage from Hemingway's *A Farewell to Arms:*

I pulled and twisted his legs loose finally and turned around and touched him. It was Passini and when I touched him he screamed. His legs were toward me and I saw in the dark and the light that they were both smashed above the knee. One leg was gone and the other was held by tendons and part of the trouser and the stump twitched and jerked as though it were not connected. (55)

As the two contrasting passages reflect, the dominant narrative strategy of Hemingway's First World War novel includes a narrator who functions to objectively communicate the environment and the images of war. In contrast, the passage from Heinemann gives us no such stable ground from which to understand the environment or the images of war. Instead, he gives us a disturbing series of images and a language that is part colloquial ("swapped"), part slang ("zips"), part formal ("lay us lengthwise") part jargon ("ciphered"), and part poetic (couldn't dig a hole deep enough, fast enough, couldn't crawl under something thick enough"). The difference between the two passages is formal. The Heinemann passage emphasizes a narrator who seems to have no stable language with which to convey experience and no objective position from which to narrate events: "We don't know," "that peculiar look around that travels from victim to victim," "our rifles and whatnot," "the scruff of the shirt, so to speak," whereas the Hemingway passage emphasizes a narrator who nearly disappears in order to give us the impression that the facts speak objectively and accurately for themselves: "His legs were toward me," "I saw in the dark and the light that they were both smashed."

Furthermore, like "Daguerre's first go with a camera obscura" (*Paco's Story* 10), it is through the movement of image followed by arresting image that *Paco's Story* blinks by. For example, the above image is followed by an image of the massacred Alpha Company, which is in turn followed by an entire series of images with an enormous range. The variety nearly reminds one of channels being flipped, ranging from a "Jesus revival meeting," to a "new car," to a "slab of plastic," to "wonder-struck Boy Scouts," to "horny sailors," to a couple of mechanics sitting around reading skin magazines. All of these images appear in less than five pages. One of the next images appears within the scene in which the medic who eventually found Paco is telling his story, years later, in a bar. In other words, the objective communication of the environment of war is being replaced by the random accumulation of images and the random accumulation of stories, not unlike the ordered yet undifferentiated stream of images characteristic of television. From this point on in my discussion I will refer to the accumulation of images and stories as a narrative strategy whereby images and narrative fragments are placed in quick and repetitive succession. The structure produced from such strategies of accumulation is a continuous series, endlessly repeatable.

A study of the use of repeated images reveals that visual authority, or the ability to trust what one sees, is also breaking down. Photography serves as an important example here. Earlier war novelists assumed that the camera that helped them to document the war experience was a neutral and objective instrument. The narrator, like the camera, could reproduce accurately information and images frame by frame. But since the 1960s, as Susan Sontag has pointed out, the photograph has been understood as an apt metaphor for how our understanding of reality is "produced" through conventions such as depth of field, angle of vision, selection of focus, type of film and development, and light readings. The visual authority of the camera as a documentary tool underwrote the assumption that we could know reality through a neutral mediation between the text and the world. Contemporary notions in literature, photography and language each propose that reality is a sign system implicated in the same endlessly deferred process of meaning production as literary texts. In each case, photographic and literary production, reality is now understood as "constructed." Visual authority and literary authority are breaking down in the Vietnam novel, because their constructedness is emphasized rather than hidden.

But these formal experiments are not without their interpretive costs. If traditional views of language, representation, and meaning are breaking down, then one could argue that *anything* written would already be unstable, or, incapable of directing narrative. This is precisely the case in *Paco's Story*, where the accumulation of random images and stories actually turns the narrative reflexively back on itself and keeps the narrative from developing. Each time the narration approaches the theme of war it will be interrupted with either another image, another story, or another form of representation. Any one of the seven chapters can in fact stand as a model for the rest of the novel. For instance, chapter three begins with Paco riding on a bus after he has returned home. Described as hunched over, cramped, sore, drugged and with a suffocating discomfort that no amount of exercises or therapies can assuage, Paco's image gives way to the memories of the bus driver as he sees the faces behind him in his rear view mirror, then to the memories of an old black woman passenger who looks at Paco and is reminded instantly of her son, then the image of Paco left at a bus stop and back again to the image of Paco at the field hospital when he was first wounded. Each image is undercut by the next image, as if no single image has any more weight than another. Similarly, each story is undercut by another, for all of the images I just mentioned carry with them a fragmented story. The continual accumulation of images and stories kill the plot and distort the theme. The ambiguous nature of Paco's story, as it continually gives way, obscures the war. The narrative position of the war hero who might transmit the story gives way as well. The war story has lost its traditional bearings; as the bus driver asserts, Paco is distinct from the figures of Korea or World War II: "If this was Korea, 1953, he'd be pushing up daisies; if this was summer, 1945, he'd have been long gone" (39). In other words, Paco is unique in part because he survived— he is the corpse that didn't get left behind. However, the hero's seat is no longer available.

The loss of the war hero position—a lost position I am now speaking of as a formal feature historically specific to the Vietnam period—can be further evidenced by looking at the way syntactic doublings and accumulations mirror the image and story accumulations I have pointed to. By syntactic doubling I mean the arrangement of words and phrases that double one another from one passage to the next, in a random order. In order to trace the syntactic versions of thematic material one must scrutinize whether or not their repetition has any narrative value. To do that one could begin anywhere in the novel. However, I will keep with the scene on the bus for the sake of clarity. For instance, the phrase "the bus driver looks full in the mirror at the many faces looking back at him" (34) is doubled a bit later in the narrative when Paco describes his surroundings after he is wounded: "the colors and shadows crisp and vivid, as radiant and sharp as a bright and interesting face in a clean mirror" (48). The events are out of chronological order (Paco's description is a memory), but the narrative gives them a different order based on the repetition of words and a kind of syntactic doubling. Similarly, descriptions of people and things merge and repeat themselves, out of narrative time but consistent with a pattern of syntactic repetition and doubling.

For example, in what reads as a remarkable section of time, word and image slippages, the passengers on the bus are described as sleepwalkers in the same way that, later, thunderheads viewed from a chopper in Vietnam are described as sleepwalkers. The rain-soaked rice paddy terrain in Vietnam is doubled by blood that soaks and floods everything in the hospital where he recovers. Similarly, Paco's tears drown his swollen mouth and the wounds that won't suture shut in a lifetime. All are linked by the descriptive term "flooded." The stripping of the cloth stuck to Paco's wounds in the medi-vac hospital is described as "almost a caress," and a caress is repeated in an image of a nurse dressing Paco's wounds at the Army hospital and at the end of the chapter when Paco slips into a memory of childhood: "the firm caresses of his father rubbing his back" (58). A "nagging, warm tingling in his legs and hips" (35) describes Paco's body on the verge of falling asleep during the bus ride. The words (and images) come back when he remembers himself slipping off his 80-100 pound rucksack pack in the jungle: "that instantly dumb, numb, inexpressible relief . . . your whole torso tingled and throbbed, ached and itched—like a foot and leg asleep" (51). The phrases "let's haul ass" (the bus driver), "Just keep hauling ass" (the chopper pilots), "let's fucking move it" (Paco wounded and waiting to be either dead or rescued) and "flying full-bore flat-out . . . to haul our asses outta there" (Paco's description of the chopper ride to the field hospital) each echo one another, as well as help to define the main character's insolubility: "Paco is in constant motion" (35). Bodies of the wounded are described as "jerking and gasping," echoed at least syntactically by hospital machines that are "hissing and thunking" and a chopper that "jerked and swung and vibrated" (56). The sun and blood both "glisten" repeatedly. As if to underscore the ceaselessly returning images and phrases that work like refrains, twice in chapter three, as in numerous instances of

Vietnam and Narrative Reflexivity

songs, signs, and slogans in other chapters, the rhythms of images and words are interrupted by song lyrics, once from soldiers parodying a patriotic war song, and once in a memory Paco has of his father singing him to sleep as a child.

Like the accumulating images in the novel, the repetition of like words or syntactic doublings that indiscriminately describe different scenes are the other side of an aesthetic spectacle of violence featured in the photographs and television clips that preceded Heinemann's novel. What makes them different is their isolation or dislocation from any specific title or commentary or description that might give them meaning. For instance, Paco imagines the headline about his ordeal will read: "F.B. HARRIETTE WIPED OUT/EXCLUSIVE PHOTOGRAPHS/SECURITY VOWS MORE TROOPS" (31), but in the novel his story never gets a caption or a headline that adequately covers his experience.

If we go back to the idea with which this chapter began, that is, that soldiers returning from Vietnam were confronted with a set of images and representations that broadcast the show of war, complete with commentary, we can compare Heinemann's use of images and commentary to the war famous in part for "coming into our living rooms." What Heinemann sets up in each chapter is a series of fundamentally illegible images and words—illegible because endlessly repeatable and interchangeable—that show us what it looks like when the themes of war have given way to the forms that are used to represent it. In such a world words and things are confused, narrative development is endlessly interrupted, and images repeat themselves without providing any meaningful teleological result. By focusing on narrative reflexivity and the accumulation of random images and syntactic doublings, *Paco's Story* effectively deconstructs the myth of an accessible experience available through language on which the First World War novel relied. The very process of writing and reading the war story dissolves the theme of war.

If we temporarily project the war novel paradigm that Fussell uses out on to our plain of reading—first, a sinister or absurd preparation, second, the unmanning experience of battle, and third, the retirement from the line to a contrasting (usually pastoral) scene where quiet meditation is allowed—and then superimpose Heinemann's story on to it what results is a representational war. I use the word war in order to suggest that the two stories are competing for meaning. Put another way, Heinemann is challenging the discursive possibility of the war story by destabilizing the conventions with which it is ordinarily built. By giving us successive images that point to themselves and confuse words with things, by dissolving the position of the narrator, and by turning the act of writing and reading the war story itself into a crisis, Heinemann relocates war at the level of representation as opposed to reality or history. The conflict emphasized in *Paco's Story* is not the Vietnam war. It is the destructive nature of the war story itself, as if Heinemann has located an error in representation and tries to make that error in representation the subject of his novel. What we are given then is a sort of refusal to develop the plot, the narrator, or the theme in favor of holding open a set of narrative questions.

Another uncomfortable example of the reflexivity that marks so many of the passages in the novel concerns the representation of wounding and killing and the actions of wounding and killing as they are conflated with the machines of killing:

> Guys're dropping like flies, Jack—horrible fuckin' heat exhaustion, ordinary ambushes, sniper fire, Chicom claymore mines as big as tractor tires, dumbfuck firefight heroes. Guys with their heads cracked open like walnuts, bleeding from the ears and the scalp. Guys with their chest squashed flat from fuckin'-A booby-trapped bombs. Guys with their legs blown off at the thighs, and shrapnel hits from there on up from a direct hit with a Chicom RPG—an armor-piercing rocket-propelled grenade. Shit! Mean and evil blood all over everything . . . (21)

Formally, the words don't particularly point to anything but themselves, to images of flesh and bomb that reflect only the total saturation of narrative and experience with violence. Legs and thighs merge with Chicom mines and shrapnel, blood from the ears and scalp comes from too many enemies: heat, ambushes, snipers, booby-traps, bombs, shrapnel, grenades. This "passage" about war is more accurately described as an instance of narrative reflexivity. The narrative cannot adequately point to something outside of itself, because the language undercuts any attempt at transcending it. In fact, as the narrative continues, it fails to provide a description that can deliver anything to the reader but more failures:

> I'd wrap the sons-a-bitches up and shoot them up, whispering 'Naw, you aint gonna die,' you poor dumb fucker. 'Trust me!' and they'd smile right back at me, 'Thanks,' like they really believed that bull-shit line, and then their eyes would roll back into their heads ('Thanks'), and their heads would roll back on their shoulders ('Thanks'), and they'd pass out from shock and die before a dust-off medevac chopper could haul-ass out to us. And the captain would be having one of his famous conniption fits, screaming some gibberish nonsense into the radio; then he'd get pissed and throw the microphone down and kick it, and he'd throw his hat down and kick it. 'These goddamn people are holding up this whole fuckin' war!' he'd say, meaning the dust-off choppers. (21)

How can we read the repetition of the word "Thanks" except reflexively, against itself? The only reading that suggests itself is one in which the content of the passage is subordinated to its language. In other words, one must read for the conflicting language of a narrative that is saturated with violence against the narrative that is supposed to represent that violence. If we read the passage, for instance, against Hemingway's *A Farewell to Arms*, what we get is an ironic twist on the idea that the soldier has learned through the sacrifice of war that he must recuperate some higher, moral meaning. With moral meaning adrift, the "Thanks" produce hollow echoes that bounce off the walls of the passage. In the above passage the dead and wounded are reduced to corpses with as little meaning as a redundant "Thanks" to no one for nothing, or the microphone thrown down and kicked, or the choppers that remain ambiguously in the service of and in the way of war. The war wounded and their place in the story have no higher meaning. They are simply one in a list of objects: plastic forks, bodies, microphones, choppers, and words. A wounded soldier has no more significance than a word. In the tension between those two readings we find the deconstruction of one story with another, the gap between signs and referents, and the failure of narrative to recuperate symbolic order or meaning. The meaning that does emerge emphasizes the importance of a lie coming apart.

Earlier I sketched out how, in Heinemann, a character's narrative authority loses its signifying power. No longer the soldier authority, Paco's voice is de-centered and dislocated. In fact, when Paco's wounded body serves as a model for reading in the opening scene, his body is almost too present. Readers must ask what the shift in emphasis, from the authority of the main character to images of his body, has to tell us. In her book *The Body in Pain: The Making and Unmaking of the World*, Elaine Scarry argues that in discussions of power and conflict, "those with power are said to be 'represented' whereas those without power are 'without representation.'" She describes the historical power relationship between the represented and the unrepresented body as follows:

> To have no body is to have no limits on one's extension out into the world; conversely, to have a body made emphatic by being continually altered through various forms of creation, instruction (e.g., bodily cleansing), and wounding, is to have one's sphere of extension contracted down to the small circle of one's immediate physical presence. Consequently, to be intensely embodied is the equivalent of being unrepresented and is almost always the condition of those without power. (207)

In Scarry's terms the soldier's body in *Paco's Story* is at war with its symbolic rivals. That is, the dismembered, angry, bloody half-corpse images that haunt the novel are in a struggle with the symbolic war story through which a soldier-hero is supposed to emerge. The demands of the body and the demands of the traditional war story no longer meet, but stand in contradiction to one another. For instance, as the narrator tells James, there is no way for Paco to explain his war wounds. He is forever confronted with the gap between the experience recorded on his body, and the words and stories available to describe it:

> [Paco] has dwelt on it with trivial thoroughness, condensed it, told it as an ugly fucking joke (the whole story dripping with iconic contra- diction, and

sarcastic and para-doxical bitterness); he's told it stone drunk to other drunks; to high-school buddies met by the merest chance (guys Paco thought he was well rid of, and never thought he'd see the rest of his natural life); to women waiting patiently for him to finish his telling so they could get him into bed, and see and touch all those scars for themselves. There's been folks whom he's unloaded the whole nine yards, the wretched soul-deadening dread, the grueling, grinding shitwork of being a grunt (the bloody murder aside); how he came to be wounded, the miracle of his surviving the massacre—as good as left for dead, you understand, James. . . . Paco (standing next to a table stacked with old stero-scope slides of St. Petersburg and Khartoum, Lisbon and San Francisco) immediately distills all that down to a single, simple sentence, squares himself (standing straight as he can), looks the old man full in the face, and says bluntly, "I was wounded in the war." (*Paco's Story* 73)

In this passage we find what Scarry might describe as a deeply, indeed almost inescapably embodied man, a body made emphatic by being continually altered through wounding. The consequence of being intensely embodied and continually altered in this manner is, according to Scarry, to be unrepresented, to be left out of culturally sanctioned forms of signification. Paco is unrepresented, and a single phrase stands in for the trauma of war: "I was wounded in the war." As the soldier's body, once a sign for a country's power and morality, is dislocated from the myths it used to sustain, that body is jettisoned from its signifying realm: John Wayne's bodily strength is replaced by Jon Voigt's or Tom Cruise's paralyzed body, for example, a demasculinized and tormented figure with a deformed story. The moral authority exemplified by John Wayne's bodily strength is also challenged.

However, it is not just male bodies that I want to track. The refusal of development figured by the narrator and in the structure of the novel finds its strongest form in the dissolution of the male body into discursive operations. The male authority inherent in the soldier is missing from *Paco's Story* because the narrator is never actually present in the story. However, the memory of Paco's body in its various forms is endlessly present in scenes of wounding. In fact, one could argue that a total dissolution of the male body is represented in the accumulation of images of Paco's body under attack:

everything smelling of ash and marrow and spontaneous combustion; everything—dog tags, slivers of meat, letters from home, scraps of sandbags and rucksacks and MPC scrip, jungle shit and human shit—everything hanging out of the woodline looking like so much rust- colored puke." (*PS*, 15-16)

Bodies, meat, letters, metal, bones, shit and puke pile on top of one another indiscriminately, marking a radical difference from the past war novel in terms of the narrative forms used to describe the experience of the soldier. Gone is the moral accounting of older forms of war storytelling, the para-

Vietnam and Narrative Reflexivity 27

digms of innocence lost and regained through battle, the wounded soldier as an allegory for the sacrifices necessary in a just war. In its place we have a narrative that fails to register any distinctions between words and things or any meaning other than itself. The above passage "lists" objects, including body parts, indiscriminately, like an undifferentiated stream of objects and moments. Similar reflexivity is registered in descriptions of Paco from the medic who found him:

> But why he wasn't dead was any body's guess. I didn't know, and I didn't want to know. He looked up at me, trying to be friendly somehow or other. And he knew he was fucked-up royal. His legs were so torn up, like someone would snap twigs for kindling, that the sons-a-bitchin dust-off medics slipped him into a spare body bag to save everything but his asshole—though he still had his cock and his balls, you understand. And the rest of him looked like someone had taken after him with one of those long-handled mallets you tenderize meat with. (24-25)

Like the assessment of the captain who gazes around the carnage at Fire Base Harriet and thinks, "This is a mean and ugly way to die and a rotten goddamn fucking piece of luck to be sure" (24), the medic's description slips from corpse to twigs to meat. What is remarkable about these passages is not that the descriptions slide around, it is that these same images and descriptions will come again in the descriptions of the Vietnamese girl's rape. Images and phrases that surface in the rape scene such as "his big meaty hand" (180) "ground the girl into rubble" (180), "snap splinters of bone" (183) and blood spattered dust are doubled in scenes describing Paco's wounded body: "mallets you tenderize meat with" and "snap twigs for kindling." What we are left with is the accumulation of images and words that refer not to some specific meaning, specific to Paco's injuries or specific to the Vietnamese girl's rape, but to their interchangeability. As the novel endlessly doubles images and syntactic operations, nearly all the descriptive passages become reflexive.

Further study of the male body read against the story of the soldier proves that Paco's body and story have a unique relationship to one another. His body—both present and absent—literally wears his story in a "mosaic of scars." Similarly, the narrative is continually interrupted by images of wounded bodies. Aside from all the images of wounded bodies, there are multiple images of feminine bodies and demasculinized male bodies. For example, when Paco is in the hospital after the war, he is "washed like an infant" before surgery. When a colonel visits him and sees Paco's massive scars, he whispers something in Paco's ear. The colonel's whisper repeats the image of Paco of his father tucking him in as a child: "It is the kiss he cherished and the memory of a whispered word" (59). Later, Paco is described in a characteristically feminized role, at the sink washing dishes. Some of the only relief from his traumatic memories comes when he washes dishes at the sink of the Texas Lunch: "reaching around, dipping his hand into the last of the greasy bus pans for the next thing to soak and scrub and rinse clean, until everything is done, and dry" (136). It is only in these "disguised" moments, disguised as an infant, a child, a woman, that Paco feels relief from the violence of his memories.

The reading I am suggesting here calls for a radical revision in our understanding of narrative and of war. The difficulty of a man unable to recognize himself or a reader unable to locate a soldier each register the ways in which Paco does not fit a symbolic position written for him by culture. The scars left on the bodies of men register a different version of masculinity than previous war stories allowed, one in which a male body is dissolving: "When the motherfuckers hit we didn't go "poof" of a piece; rather, we disappeared like sand dunes in a stiff and steady offshore ocean breeze—one goddamned grain at a time" (16). That dissolving male body is not one we have yet accounted for. A strange example of a zoom-lens look at Paco's body suggests just such a reading:

> If we could lean down and take a good hard look, and see all that, James, even in this little light. We could back away, now that we know what we are looking at, and those scars will seem to wiggle and curl, snapping languidly this way and that, the same and grubs and crawlers when you prick them with the barb of a bait hook. But it is only an illusion, James, a sly trick of the eye—the way many frightful things in this world come alive in the dimmest, whitest moonlight, the cleanest lamplight. (171)

It is as if Heinemann can only hang on to a male body by finding different disguises for it. Here we are reading "a sly trick of the eye," an error if you will, revealing a disguised masculine body. This male body is covered with scars like worms and snakes that are not ordinarily readable. Perhaps other "frightful things" such as war and even male violence only "come alive" in the dimmest light. In other words, perhaps the male body disguised by scars points us toward stories ordinarily repressed.

It is that repressed story, ordinarily hidden beneath the story of the male soldier and male violence that comes into question when we read bodies in *Paco's Story*. In terms of violence, the horror of the bloody massacre at Fire Base Harriet is challenged by the gruesome gang rape scene in the novel. The thematic stability of the rape sequence in the novel is as difficult to decipher as the war memories, because it is rendered unstable by a set of voyeurism scenes that duplicate its images and descriptive operations. I have already suggested that the primary rape scene in the novel reflects the narrative patterns of other passages in the novel, particularly the accumulation of images and syntactic doublings. I am now suggesting that the treatment of Paco's wounded body and the raped body follow the same formal patterns. Paco's wounded body prefigures the violence of the novel; it shows us how to read the narrative reflexively, against itself. Heinemann teaches us to read images on top of images, words as interchangeable, and scenes as endlessly repeat-

Vietnam and Narrative Reflexivity

able. There are three scenes of violence in which victim and victimizer are confused. Each is predicated on the image and description of Paco's wounded body that opens the novel. They are: the actual rape of a Vietnamese sniper girl during the war, the figurative rape of Cathy through Paco's voyeurism, and the figurative rape of Paco in Cathy's voyeurism and sexual fantasies, recorded in her diary. Drawing from my argument about reflexivity, I would now like to chart how the three scenes of violence confuse victim with victimizer, because they are formally mixed-up with one another in terms of image and syntax.

This reading is not a common one, especially among feminist critics, most of whom argue that Heinemann's novel participates in sustaining those values of patriarchy that underwrite male violence. For instance, in her book *The Remasculinization of America*, Susan Jeffords argues that the representational forms of the Vietnam War "are structurally written through relations of gender" (xi). In her reading of *Paco's Story*, Jeffords charges the rape scene involving the Viet Cong sniper girl (the only "real" rape she finds in the story) with being one of the harshest scenes in all of Vietnam literature and goes on to claim that Paco's struggle (and by extension Heinemann's) throughout the novel is to forget or repress this gang-rape.

I make a different argument that resists reading Paco as a rapist and masculine violence as implicitly enforced through Paco's desire. In particular it is the issue of voyeurism and its connection to formal narrative strategies that complicates *Paco's Story*. More specifically, Heinemann represents looking, both in the camera eye sense and in the human eye sense, as an act of violence.

Developing that argument first requires a reading of the rape of a Vietnamese sniper who has taken the lives of two American soldiers:

> And when Gallagher finished, Jonesy fucked her, and when Jonesy was done, half the fucking company was standing in line and commenced to fuck her ragged . . . watching one another while they ground the girl into the rubble. . . . Dudes still ambled over to the doorway to watch, to call out coaching, taking their turns, hanging around the side of the building after—some getting back in line. (180-81)

Gallagher has tied the woman's arms with wire looped over the beam of a bombed-out structure and shoved her onto a table covered with "chunks of tiles and scraps of air-burst howitzer shrapnel" (180). Paco remembers her bowels "squeezing as tight as if you were ringing out a rag," (180–81), and he comments to James that he can see the "huge red mark in the middle of her back" (181) where Gallagher pressed his hand. After the gang rape Gallagher shoots her in the head. The important images and words to take note of include: "ragged," "ringing out a rag," "ground into rubble," "chunks and scraps" and the meaty hand in the middle of her back. If we now recall the phrases from the medic's description of Paco, an eerie repetition emerges:

"mallets you tenderize meat with." The other images loom like incoming as we read on.

A second layer of development focuses on a close reading of voyeurism. One of Paco's activities while on break at the Texas Lunch is voyeurism. He watches a young girl named Cathy at the Geronimo Hotel:

> Well, one night the lights in the front apartment of the Geronimo Hotel suddenly catch his eye. And Paco sees a young woman with fuzzy blond hair parading around in threadbare cotton underwear, bra and underpanties. . . . Paco sits on that stoop in the alley with the cigarette smoke hot on the back of his hand, watching up at her that night and many another night. (146)

One could easily read Paco's voyeurism as an example of the violence implicit in Paco's violent, male desire. However, the evidence for a different reading happens when one observes how the repetition of words and images from the rape come back in scenes of voyeurism. One important act of voyeurism that echoes Paco's and the rape cannot be ignored. Cathy, the flirtatious young girl who Paco meets working at the Texas Lunch, observes Paco without his permission. Between them they create a sort of "game" of looking:

> He stretches this way and that, listening to the pins and screws in his legs grating. The damp work pants pull at his knees; his wrinkly feet squish in his shoes. He has his juice jar and cigarette and a "strike anywhere" match, and glances up at the girl's windows (her name, Cathy, James, student at the Wyandotte Teacher's College west of town, and niece to Earl and Myrna). He sees her, dressed in that threadbare underwear of hers, pull up a chair near the window and sit deeply down, and stare into the back doorway of the Texas Lunch. (147)

As if to underscore the message, Paco's aside to James finishes the scenes: "For weeks now James, Cathy would turn off all the lights in her apartment, pull a bentwood chair got from downstairs to the middle of the room, and sit, slouching just so—tranquil and patient—barely able to see over the windowsill. . . It is quite a game she plays, James, spying on him at work" (148). In these passages we are inside Paco's imagination, a conversation we are only barely privy to, if one considers the displaced voice of the narrator. However, another account of voyeurism represents the violence from earlier scenes, and curiously, that violence happens in *Cathy's* version, not Paco's. Cathy's diary describes a violent sexual fantasy with Paco:

> He holds himself up, stiff armed, and arches his back and reaches up to his forehead and begins by pinching the skin there, but he's working the skin loose, and then he begins to peel the scars off as if they were a mask. It's as if he's unbuttoning the snaps of a jacket. Like you'd see someone pull up dried spaghetti from a kitchen table. He held the scars in his fist as if they

were a spool of twine tangled in a terrible knot . . . he's holding me down with that hard belly of his, and lays the scars on my chest . . . I could hear the stitches ripping. (208-9)

This is the place where a deferral of one reading can lead to a deeper understanding of the way images and syntactic structures double one another throughout the novel to produce their own meaning. In Cathy's diary images and words from the rape of the Viet Cong girl such as "zipping up a parka" resurface as "stitches ripping" and "buttoning the snaps of a parka." Rape terms and voyeurism terms are mixed up with one another: "he's holding me down." Cathy watches Paco "drive his knuckles into his back" (146) from fatigue at the Texas Lunch, doubling the phrase and the image that Paco watched of Gallagher "pressing his meaty hand into the middle of her back" (180) during the rape. In the rape scene, the sound that the Vietnamese girl's body makes against the table is described as "the way you might pound on a kitchen table with the heel of your hand" (181) leaving a "huge red mark [is left] in the middle of her back" (181). In Cathy's diary she describes Paco's shirt as a "gray sodden rag" (204), and during the rape the girl is "fucked ragged" and her bowels are squeezed tight "as if you were ringing out a rag" (181). The Viet Cong girl and Paco both "cry hysterically." Paco and the Viet Cong girl are described as being pulverized by "chunks and slivers" that grind into their flesh. In other words, images and syntactic doublings from the gang rape appear in the original description of Paco's body after he is burned and wounded, as well as in Cathy's diary entries. The narrative uncomfortably conflates the images and words from the three scenes—Paco's wounded body, the rape, Cathy's voyeurism—so that we remember them from one to the next. The almost unbearably repetitive passages stand in place of any clear narrative meaning that would distinguish between rape, war wounds, and voyeurism. In such a territory, victim and victimizer are not stable positions; representation itself is in crisis.

There is far more formal narrative evidence to associate the Viet Cong girl with Paco than with Cathy. For like Paco, she is combat-experienced, and she is described as having a "flat, mannish face" (184). Similarly, her ravenous hunger "wolfing down a C-ration can of ham and eggs some fucked-up guy had given her" (175) parallels Paco's ravenous hunger for chili the first time he enters the Texas Lunch. They are both hard workers, "by the look of her back she had worked, *hard*, every day of her life" (174), and the twine she is tied with during the gang rape recurs throughout Paco's nightmares in images of twine, rope and tangled knots. And just as the Viet Cong girl is "ground . . . into rubble" (180), so too is Paco pulverized by the Fire Base Harriet incident. Lastly, the room in which the girl is gang raped contains a raw wood table described as being like a "kitchen table" (179, 181). Kitchen tables appear in Paco's dreams, in descriptions of his workplace after the war, and in Cathy's diary entries. It is possible that Paco and the Vietnamese rape victim are two casualties of war, one written atop the other, in spite of our discomfort at reading them as such. In other words, war as a paradigm of masculine violence and rape as a form of masculine violence are both underwritten by a third story, the dissolving body of the Vietnam soldier who is the freakish object of scrutiny, voyeurism, fantasy and hate.

But the scenes of voyeurism and the rape scenes are even more complex. One reading would seem to posit that the payback for Fire Base Harriette's massacre caused by friendly fire is the total destruction of a Viet Cong girl. This would indeed leave a reader to deduce that the spectacle of masculine violence in its larger sense is figured by rape. But if the story is about reading, as I have argued, the rape would need to be read *against* its figurative implications. Because the rape is disturbingly represented as "beautiful and terrible" (177), it reflects something about its reception as well as the complicity of a reader. That is, since the novel *emphasizes* that war can be represented either beautifully or terribly, and rape can be represented either beautifully or terribly, and voyeurism beautifully or terribly, it asks us to consider whether or not reading carries with it the same options. Clearly the author wants us to take some time to struggle with this question. Our shock does not only register our moral recoil; it registers our complicity.

It is with this notion of a reader's complicity that I end my discussion. In this novel, the juxtaposition and repetition of images works against a set of more culturally authorized stories. Instead of reading Paco as the war soldier who witnesses and tries to communicate violence, we might read Paco as the discursive figure of a dissolving authority. Similarly, instead of reading Paco as the male aggressor and Cathy and the Vietnamese girl as feminine victims, we might read Paco as the discursive figure of war's wounds, and Cathy as the discursive figure of an audience who watched the war at home on their televisions with nothing less than voyeuristic fascination. That voyeuristic fascination, according to Heinemann, is unbearably violent. In this case Cathy is symbolically punished for her voyeurism by having the scars of the war burned into her flesh, and Paco is demasculinized to the point of a dissolution of the male body into narrative, literally drowned by words. However, I am not suggesting a thematic reading in which we pity rather than condemn the soldier. This war story is unrepresentable, and that fundamental mark of illegibility informs the structure of the entire novel. The novel charts the failure of narrative to write Paco or war. What we gain when we give up a mimetic relation between language and experience is the chance to restructure the experience of war—it is not naturally given, but open to interpretation.

Soon after Paco finds and reads Cathy's diary he leaves town, unable to bear himself observed and written: "He doesn't want to read anymore, flips the diary shut and sits up, puts the chair back where it was . . ." and leaves (209). What we are left with is representational, or more precisely, a lost theme, a dissolved character, and a pile of images and empty forms. Before Paco leaves he writes:

*Thanks for the
work. Got to
go. See you
around.*
    Paco (209)

No Paco, no war, just endlessly exchangeable signs. This last observation has deep political and historical implications, especially since Heinemann has dislocated "Vietnam" from its specifically political and historical markers. What would happen if we lost Vietnam? I will conclude with the claim that Vietnam is already an eerie set of texts, including films, memoirs, oral histories, the names on the Memorial in Washington, news articles and books, archives, State Department documents and political policies, television images and protest slogans. These are the forms by which citizens, soldiers, and authors have access to that war. *Paco's Story* takes us to a place where words are breaking down and meaning hangs contingent on overlapping images and stories. Even as we begin to close the factual book on the event, our political and historical definitions of "Vietnam" sit poised there, fundamentally open to narrative possibilities.

NOTES

1. Fussell appears to be arguing for a specific version of a more general argument made by Lévi-Strauss concerning the narrative nature of all historiography: "In spite of worthy and indispensable efforts to bring another moment of history alive and to possess it, a clairvoyant history should admit that it never completely escapes from the nature of myth." See Lévi-Strauss, "Overture to *Le Cru et le cuit*" in *Structuralism*, 33-55. Fussell argues that our entire cultural understanding of history and particularly of war is based on specifically literary forms. Fussell argues that, in effect, even participants of war have no other "access" to their experience, since the experience itself is beyond the scope of human expression.

2. While I will not provide a detailed analysis of these novels, I will use Hemingway as a formal instance of the First World War novel in which the goal was to describe what those who did not experience the war could not imagine, and to recover some sense of higher, moral meaning from the chaos and wounds of war.

CHAPTER III
War as Narrative Discourse

BY TURNING TO ENGLISH NOVELIST DORIS LESSING'S SCIENCE FICTION WORK *SHIKASTA*, readers can both locate and dislocate Vietnam as a historical marker. As several critics have pointed out, Lessing does not present Vietnam as the war that confirms a pattern of generational violence (Hanley 115; Sullivan, 160–61). Lessing's generation was born into war and came of age during war, and her work in particular points to the development of a whole series of wars that constructed a pattern of violence extending up and through many generations. For example, Lessing's parents were a World War I amputee and his nurse, and she grew up during World War II, thus a certain story of war and violence was handed down in her own family. According to Lessing in *A Small Personal Voice*, the idea of her *Children of Violence* series was to write "about people like myself, people my age who are born out of wars and who live through them, the framework of lives in conflict" (57). In *Children of Violence*, Lessing tells the story of war as a family legacy. The series focuses on World War I and World War II and closes the gap, through narrative, between the battle front and the home front. In *Shikasta*, all wars, including Vietnam, are stripped of their special historical and national status and written into a pattern of global violence with causes that go beyond the limits of warring nations.

Like the extra-galactic extended viewpoint from which *Shikasta* emerges, Lessing fashions a wide and impersonal view of war and violence of the last 100 years. At the heart of her sci-fi fantasy is the question: how do we remember ourselves through war, or, how do we make stories of ourselves from within cultures saturated by the memory of war? In this chapter I will focus on how the changing memory and place of war are connected to narrative form by analyzing what I call Lessing's dialogic form. By dialogic form I mean the generation of a constant interaction between meanings that interferes with absolute or authoritative meaning. Partly I am constructing this definition through the work of M. M. Bakhtin in *The Dialogic Imagination*. In particular, his use of the term "dialogism" refers to a system in which there is a perpetual interaction between meanings. Dialogized language is aware of competing definitions for meaning and undialogized language is authoritative and unitary. In Bakhtin's terms, Lessing's novel emphasizes what he claims about novelistic discourse in general, that is, that it undoes the idea that language is unified and meaning absolute, since it allows for the variety of social and historical conditions surrounding a text to achieve articulation. But what I am arguing about Lessing in particular is that her formal experiments, the mixing of discourses and kinds of knowledge, are set into a motion particular to her style and topic. That is, her style is to disrupt binary oppositions and leave recognizable arguments unresolved or dissolved, and her topic is war as a model of social organization. I will trace Lessing's dialogic form through the over-arching structure of the novel, the mixing of religious, political and scientific discourses with novelistic narrative, the juxtaposition of physical and psychic worlds, and the disruption of a traditional protagonist/antagonist character schema. The term "discourse," as I use it here, means a subdivision of language given authority and privilege by the dominant culture, such as legal discourse, religious discourse, and so on. However, I will also show how Lessing, like Foucault, who is most immediately connected to contemporary understandings of the term "discourse," undercuts that definition by presenting history as a set of competing discourses.

Like many of the novels in Lessing's literary career, the *Canopus in Argos* series reflects her deep conviction that war extends beyond the battlefield. The theme of a never-ending violence is played out in her *Children of Violence* series, and in her collection of essays, *Prisons We Choose to Live Inside*. For example, in her series about World War I and World War II, *Children of Violence*, Lessing writes about war as an inherited family trait, and with similar methods, in *Prisons We Choose to Live Inside*, she reminds us that our dread of war is complex, as it includes a secret excitement:

> In my time I have through many many hours of listening to people talking about war, the prevention of war, the awfulness of war, with it never once being mentioned that for large numbers of people the idea of war is exciting, and that when war is over they may say it was the best time in their lives. This may be true even of people whose experiences of war were terrible, and which ruined their lives. People who have lived through a war know that as it approaches, an at first secret unacknowledged elation begins, as if an almost inaudible drum is beating . . . an awful, illicit, violent excitement is abroad. Then the elation becomes too strong to be ignored or overlooked: then every one is possessed by it. (10)

According to Lessing, deep within the complex ambiguities of our feelings about war rests a psychic battlefield already animated by our relationships to one another. She identifies and renders the theme of violence in the books of the *Canopus* series, wherein the story of war is told in terms of internal as well as external conflict. Betsy Draine, in *Substance Under Pressure*, analyzes the experimental forms of Lessing's novels and argues that Lessing breaks down the story of war over and over again in order to reach worlds of conflict informed by gender, race, and class. Similarly, critics repeatedly identify Lessing's use of "two warring worlds" as a metaphoric approach to taking apart gender binaries (Draine 149; Perrakis 221; Fishburn 60). Most criticism of Lessing's later novels and in particular the *Canopus* series focuses on the relation between science fiction and feminism. For instance, feminist studies have theorized the importance of dystopian and utopian worlds as a vehicle for critiquing gender in the works of writers such as Lessing, Ursula Le Guin (*Always Coming Home*, 1985), and Margaret Atwood (*The Handmaid's Tale*, 1986), among others. But I would like to look as *Shikasta* from the angle of post-World War II novels specifically in order to see what the war novel can show us about war and narrative.

The *Canopus in Argos* series most directly challenges post-World War II understandings of war because it deeply disturbs traditional historical accounts. In *No Man's Land: Letters From the Front*, Sandra Gilbert and Susan Gubar argue that the major difference between the literature of World War I and World War II is that the event of the Second World War marked the beginning of a "series," where the First World War marked a historical (and literary) autonomous and momentous event. With that change came a fissure in history through which women writers of war emerged, a history largely ignored in Paul Fussell's literary history of war *The Great War and Modern Memory*, which charts the expression of the experience of male soldiers and male authors (with limited mention of Virginia Woolf as contributing to the body of war literature of this century). But as Gilbert and Gubar have argued, while World War I and the years directly following were dominated by war novels by men, the years shortly before World War II and the years directly following it were dominated by war novels by women, including the wartime writings of Elizabeth Bishop, Edith Sitwell, Kay Boyle and perhaps most importantly, Virginia Woolf, as well as the postwar narratives of H.D. and Doris Lessing. For Gilbert and Gubar the war between the sexes emerged in part as a function of war in general; thus the rise of wartime writing by women has intimate connections to sexual politics between 1914 and 1950.[1]

Changes in sexual politics and in the story of war had formal effects. Unlike the pastoral remove and the modernist irony Fussell identified as the central literary trope of the literature of World War I, characteristic of novels such as *All Quiet on the Western Front*, *Goodbye to All That*, and *A Farewell to Arms*, Gilbert and Gubar argue that the literature between 1914 and 1950, particularly those works written by women, emphasizes the dislocation of war from the battlefield and the relocation of war onto fields of sexuality and other psycho-social categories, with a special set of changes in narrative form. I would like to extend that argument, particularly on the issue of form; that is, what can the forms of post World War II novels such as Lessing's tell us about the war novel and about narrative form? Contemporary scholarship on Woolf, Lessing, and other wartime women writers has broken down war as an issue of gender relations. For example, *Virginia Woolf and War: Fiction, Reality and Myth* (1991) is an excellent collection of essays that explores the variety of meanings of war in Woolf's body of work, emphasizing in particular her anti-militarism and its connection to feminism. Claire Tylee's book *The Great War and Women's Consciousness: Images of Militarism and Womanhood in Women's Writings* (1990) traces particular images of victimhood, empowerment, and militarism in World War I texts written by women; and Jean Bethke Elshtain's book *Women and War* (1987) analyzes the terms and figures of war from a feminist point of view, deconstructing the notions of "bellicose soldiers" and "passive women" in particular. Another angle on that same issue, one that analyzes the identity construction of the male soldier and the discourses that substantiated that identity would be Klaus Theweleit's *Male Fantasies* and William Gibson's *Warrior Dreams*.

In *Shikasta*, Lessing uses traditional tropes of science fiction, such as alien planets, wars between galactic empires, extraterrestrial visitors to earth, and the reporting of an alien to superiors who are in some way studying our planet. In addition, she employs a second reality based on one we recognize as our own in terms of evolution—a "subgroup of 'monkeys' had established themselves and were developing . . . showing rapid increases in intelligence" (14). She also works to trouble a reader's prior view of earth, history, or human behavior so that they can be instructed how to look at history from a more galactic viewpoint: "The planet was for millions of years one of a category of hundreds that we kept a watch on" (14). These narrative strategies are common to most if not all novels in the science fiction genre (Draine 143). In addition, science fiction as a literary genre developed alongside some key cultural factors at the turn of the century. As Betsy Draine argues in *Substance Under Pressure: Artistic Coherence and Evolving Form in the Novels of Doris Lessing*, science fiction as a form of cosmic and fictionalized history corresponded to a number of cultural factors emerging in the years between 1900-1945:

> First, public interest in science and scientific method; secondly, the secularization of knowledge that followed; third, the acceptance of the theory of evolution; an finally, the development of astronomy and public interest in the question of whether life exists beyond earth. It is thus a modern and secularized cosmogony. (147)

Early works of space travel such as H. G. Wells' *The War of the Worlds* (1897) and *The First Men in the Moon* (1901) are also counted as influences of Lessing's, as well as Edmond Hamilton's stories in the American magazine *Weird Tales*, from which Lessing borrowed the name "Canopus," and Olaf Stapledon's *Last and First Men*, (1903) a novel Lessing mentions in her preface to *Shikasta*. What science fiction affords an author is a genre in which sci-

War as Narrative Discourse

entific understandings of reality are used as a starting ground from which to explore imaginary possibilities. Lessing uses our understanding of and deep interest in space travel and alien life forms to re-tell the history of war—World War I, World War II, Vietnam, Afghanistan, and the possibility of World War III—and to explore imaginary alternatives to war in the realm of the fantastic. According to Lessing on the first page of her opening remarks to *Shikasta*, the realist novel's limits precluded the questions she was interested in:

> It is by now commonplace to say that novelists everywhere are breaking the bonds of the realistic novel because what we all see around us becomes daily wilder, more fantastic, incredible. Once, and not so long ago, novelists might have been accused of exaggerating, or dealing overmuch in coincidence or the improbable: now novelists themselves can be heard complaining that fact can be counted on to match our wildest inventions. (i)

Lessing's novel thus dislocates the theme of war from the battlefield, the realist novel and from history books and relocates it at the level of the fantastic, a narrative strategy common to many science fiction novels. That is, particular wars that have some special historical significance are displaced onto a science fiction constellation in which either there are no historical markers, historical markers have been flattened, or new markers are emerging. This kind of galactic viewpoint dissolves the special status given to individual wars and situates them instead within a larger story of perpetual violence. In particular, Lessing's *formal* influences can be charted through a group of wartime writings by women who were experimenting with form beyond the limits of modernist literary narrative features. Specifically the inclusion and scrutiny of class and gender within the textual surface of the war novel, prevalent in the works of Virginia Woolf such as *Jacob's Room, To The Lighthouse, Between the Acts* and *Three Guineas*, prove illuminating as we search for Lessing's formal influences. However, it is Lessing's focus on the history of war *and* the history of the representation of war that makes her narrative choices unique, as I will show.

Shikasta is one of the five books from the *Canopus in Argos Archives*. Each of the books projects a relationship between people and planets in some form of crisis, introduces a narrator who acts as a historical observer and a conduit for change, and juxtaposes psychic and physical worlds. All the books dislocate war, by replacing a certain model of war as combat with structures of consciousness. *The Marriage of Zones 3, 4, and 5* (1980) explores the way the relationships between people and planets are connected to their social evolution. *The Sirian Experiments* is a story wherein an archivist's account, or, more precisely, historical narrative, is revised after numerous encounters with Canopus over a long period of time. *The Making of the Representative for Planet 8* (1982) focuses on a planet like Shikasta where a cosmic accident has occurred. In this story the planet loses warmth; in *Shikasta* the planet loses its psychic strength. Both stories reveal how a people must learn or learn again who they are in order to overcome their own possible destruction. The fifth book, *Documents Relating to the Sentimental Agents in the Volyen Empire* (1983), is an example of how an historical observer can be overtaken by emotions drawn from language itself—from the telling and retelling of stories.

The narrative structure of *Shikasta* is first divided by two planetary perspectives. One vision is of Shikasta and Shikastans and focuses on the emotional and psychic evolution of the people. The other vision is from the planet Canopus which is a much larger and far-ranging perspective which includes Shikasta and other planets. In her essay "The Marriage of Inner and Outer Space in Doris Lessing's *Shikasta*" Phyllis Sternberg Perrakis argues that "the interaction between the two perspectives, the effect of each on the other, is what determines the meaning of the book" (220). But this rather simple dualism is very much complicated by the competing discourses of the novel, including reports, documents, and scientific observations from the narrator and historical officer, Johor, conflicting histories from communications between world leaders, and diary entries from Johor's friends and relatives. Thus, the relationship between perspectives demands further scrutiny, especially at the level of narrative form. These competing discourses combined with the interference, if you will, of narrative forms, work to dislocate war historically as a model of combat and relocate war as a discursive construct, as I will argue.

The first half of the novel extends to page 210, concluding in the reincarnation of Johor as the human George Sherban. The second half of the novel extends to page 365 and ends with a report post World War III. The most predominant narration is that of Johor, an envoy from Canopus, and in the second half Johor is more or less reincarnated on Shikasta as the main character, George Sherban. The most striking effect produced from this two-in-one narrator is that the reader is forced to witness two different versions or accounts of the archivist's history. Thus the basic structure of the novel is dialogic, generating a multi-layered discussion with the reader. In addition, there are two audiences in the novel, one intradiagetic and one extradiagetic. One audience consists of the inhabitants of the planet. It is Johor's mission to convince them that the planet is worth saving. The other audience is the reader, who recognizes Lessing's science fiction version of the world as echoing her own. Stuck there, the reader is offered a narrative imperative that challenges material very familiar to us. For example, readers will recognize Darwin's theories of evolution, the Golden Age myth, and the Biblical account of the Fall, rewritten in Johor's reports and experiences. In Johor's explanations of the patterns of stones set up to conduct power through the earth, the reader can easily spot Stonehenge. The Biblical Flood is rewritten as a cosmic accident resulting in a shift of the earth's axis. Other biblical material is given scientific form as well. The covenant of the ark, the wanderings of Moses, the delivery of the commandments, the fall of the tower of Babel, and the modern worship of the infant of Prague are each given a sci-

War as Narrative Discourse

entific explanation in the reports of Johor. In other words, Lessing draws from the Old Testament, the Torah, the New Testament and the Koran, among other sacred texts and transforms them into scientific data recorded in a series of reports. For example, Johor's mission is to assist in and record the progress of the evolution of life on Shikasta. Darwin's history of evolution and the history of the Fall are related as "accidents of the cosmic type," and "shifts in stellar alignments" (21) in Johor's accounts:

> The planet was for millions of years one of a category of hundreds that we kept a watch on. It was regarded as having potential because its history has always been one of sudden changes, rapid developments, as rapid degradations, periods of stagnation. Anything could be expected of it. . . . We wanted the northern hemisphere, because it was chiefly here that a subgroup of the former "monkeys" had established themselves and were developing . . . They showed rapid increase in intelligence. Our experts told us that these creatures would continue a fast evolution and could be expected to become a Grade A species in, probably, fifty thousand years (Provided of course there were no more accidents of the cosmic type). (14-15)

Lessing goes on to attribute human selfishness, hatred, and war to a variety of "cosmic accidents." Like the global accident reports, Johor's perceptions are broken and partial, inadequate and inconsistent. Sometimes they come in the form of reports, sometimes in the form of other official documents, sometimes in letters and sometimes in diary entries from people close to him. Each report is conveyed through a different system of meaning. Lessing uses typography, headings, bolding and italicizing print, and spacing shifts to signal the change from one kind of knowledge or story to the next. Shifts in perspective are reflected in shifts on the page. The "record" of history is thus equally broken up, forcing the reader to collect a variety of reports and struggle with their conflicting meanings. More importantly, those competing discourses and conflicting meanings produce their own dialogic form. It is as if Lessing is asking the reader to imagine war as discursive, a function of a set of competing discourses always emerging and simultaneously disappearing from view.

If we recast that last idea in the form of a question regarding how we remember war, we are in a similar position to Johor's but also to his audience's. We are, in other words, in a temporary or provisional position where the experience of violence and war is only available as a fragmented, half-forgotten pile of documents. *Shikasta* begins by giving us a glimpse of a moment in which war is not the dominant cultural narrative. We begin with a recollection of the main narrator, the Canopean envoy Johor, who is a member of the Canopean Colonial Service and an emissary to Shikasta. Shikasta is "the broken one," or what readers can recognize as a distorted kind of Earth. Johor's work has taken him across thousands of years, and his current mission has landed him in late twentieth-century Shikasta during "The Century of Destruction." Feeling deep ambivalence about his current mission, Johor slips into a memory of a past visit to Earth during "The First Time":

> Not in this city could it be possible for a child being brought by its parents to be introduced to the halls, towers, centers of its heritage, to feel awed and alienated, to know itself a nothing, a little frightened creature who must obey, and watch for Authority. Long sad experience had taught me to watch for this . . . but on the contrary, anyone walking here, among these welcoming warm-colored buildings, must feel only the closeness, the match, between individual and surroundings. (32)

As Paul Fussell argues, it is a common narrative strategy in war novels of this century to use the memory of a pastoral scene to evoke nostalgia for a happier, more peaceful time. For example, in *The Great War and Modern Memory* he argues that a narrative pattern based on going in and out of violence and terror to pastoral oases forms the dynamics for many World War I works. In that retreat the individual establishes what Fussell identifies as an ironic distance, a literary feature central to novels of war. For instance, in Hemingway's *A Farewell to Arms*, the hero withdaws not just to Naples but also to idyllic Capri to recover from wounds sustained in Anzio and to order the chaos of his experience in a moment of tranquility. (236-37) In the above passage from Lessing's novel, the "warm colored buildings," the "closeness," "the match between an individual and surroundings" reflect a pre-lapsarian world which has been destroyed by "Authority," "alienation," and war. But as Lynne Hanley argues in *Writing War*, often our dominant memories of war are actually very careful accounts of how we *forget*. This initial example of Johor's memory locates a cultural mistake in the interpretation of history. We remember a garden where the ruins of history are accumulating in a great pile. The difference between Hemingway's text and Lessing's is that by nature of his cosmic perspective, Johor already sees the destructive impulse within the idyllic: "And yet it was there, just audible, the faintest of discords, the beginnings of the end" (33). Johor makes this observation over and over again in his reports each time a romantic memory of the past surfaces in his mind (38; 63; 145-49). The formal option of pastoral remove is revealed as a false route to telling the truth about war. *Shikasta* begins to show us how we distance ourselves from war, how we "relegate war—and its consequences—into something that happened elsewhere and did not affect [us]; or something that had happened to [us], but between such and such dates, and then taken itself off" (232).

Lessing sets up her initial models of competing accounts of reality in order to both familiarize readers with a common historical viewpoint and defamiliarize them. Through the conventions of science fiction and through a specific use of competing discourses, readers are given a temporary position from which to view the chaotic structures of a characteristically militaristic, violent culture. In that mixing of discourses, Lessing's narrative strategies differ from World War I novelists such as Hemingway, for instance, or the war memoirist Siegfried Sasson, or the wartime poet Wilfred Owen, who focused on the soldier's experience of the front and a set of narrative conventions that supported that experience. In particular the difference rests on the way writers address the relationship between the real and the representational; it would seem that science fiction afforded Lessing a new angle of vision.

As I mentioned in previous chapters, Paul Fussell identified the archetypal literary forms of romance, irony and heroism that appear in the literature of World War I as a means for communicating the experience of the soldier at the front. More precisely, he claims that in dealing with the memory of war, participants and authors both employ "irony assisted recall" by shaping into significance an event that threatens to destroy meaning altogether—war (30).

However, Lessing's novel and especially the novels of women writers after World War II undercut the paradigm as well as the narrative forms that Fussell charted by designing worlds of war that infect the entire fabric of social existence. Gilbert and Gubar's *No Man's Land: Sex Changes*, for instance, revises the notion of a novelistic modernist irony and the soldier's heroism by subjecting those ideas to scrutiny in light of the wartime writings of women. Where Robert Graves employed the literary device of satire and the elements of stage comedy in *Goodbye to All That* in order to activate the ironic distance theorized by Paul Fussell, and where Ernest Hemingway reflected his experience as a war reporter by lending his main character this trait, women writers such as Virginia Woolf reduced narrative to pieces of plays that interrupt the narrative (*Jacob's Room*), and brackets, parentheses, and journalistic fragments (*To The Lighthouse*). The difference is that World War I writers appear to have located the war at the level of theme and understood representation as reflective of reality, and those who followed, particularly but not limited to women writers, located the war at the level of form and began to understand representation as constructing reality in a variety of ways. The breaking apart of forms that emerged, I would argue, with Virginia Woolf, produced not only a different account of war but also a different understanding of the relation between history and representation, a new understanding that had at its front issues of gender.

But in order to make the argument that Lessing's novel undercuts the paradigms and forms of the war novel outlined by Fussell, one must first understand how the disturbance of the real through competing discourses and the break-down of narrative conventions happen at the level of both the production of the text and the thematic matter of the text. For instance, earlier I claimed that Johor's memory locates a cultural mistake in the interpretation of history, in which a pastoral scene stands in for the forgetting of a war-torn history. Similarly, Lessing's emphasis on the never-ending flow of wars foregrounds the image of conflicts stacked or heaped onto history; successive wars have so piled up the power of the military and the arms industry in the novel (the thematic) that they alone prescribe the form and intensity of warfare: "Again the armament industries flourished, and [World War II] . . . finally established them as the real rulers of every geographical area" (86). Formally, this information is related either in a never-ending supply of reports either from Johor or from previous envoys, or in informal terms such as letters and diary entries, focusing on the visual cue of a report, including headings, subheadings, and "official" document titles such as "History of Shikasta," "Documents Relating to the Youth Armies," and "Additional Explanatory Information." Narrative sections that relate informal and personal perspectives, such as "RACHEL SHERBAN'S JOURNAL," are italicized. Lessing breaks down any single version that might explain which report is most accurate. In a way the reports and narrative sections disturb the notion of authorhood because each is just one in a series registered, for instance, as a "summary chapter" from "History of Shikasta, Volume 3012." In other words, the mixing of many discourses in *Shikasta* is a representational version of the way history itself evolves according to Lessing—in pieces, piles, and conflicting accounts of events. Furthermore, the event, war, is also neverending. As Johor remarks, "But there would be more, and more, and more . . . there were more and more: millions. And millions. Armies have their own momentum, logic, life" (232). A reader finds it difficult to distinguish between the theme and the work itself.

Put slightly differently, the theme is an unthinkable—because uncontainable—perpetual war, and the form of the novel mixes discourses and kinds of knowledge with narrative in an effort to emphasize the constructed nature of our experiences. In *Shikasta*, "truth" is unstable. A diary entry is represented in italics and in an informal language: "*This bit is being written several weeks later. Nine to be exact. Two facts. One is, several times I have found myself—I put it like this because it is always by accident*" (230). A page later a random section from The History of Shikasta, VOL. 3014 is represented in bold face type: "**Never was there a time on Shikasta when it was easier to see what was coming; never a time when it *could* have been so easy for them to understand the simple truth that they were not in control of what was happening to them**" (231). Add to these the positions of the narrator, who shifts perspectives from reports out of context and reports from a political set of events he participates in, as well as the position of the reader, who is forced to choose what to believe and what to throw out in terms of data, and what the reader is left with is a pile of discursive fragments, a formal answer to the chaos of war that does not rely on ordering or unifying meaning.

Lessing's novel in large part focuses attention on these competing discourses and their relationship to the workings of memory. This is one instance where the accumulation of discourses and the mixing of different forms of knowledge emerge as formal features central to Lessing's novel. Both the content of Johor's/George's reports and the formal strategy of competing discourses record how Johor is a figure caught in a fragmented memory: "I shall set down my recovered memories of my visit to Shikasta . . . I am also making use of records of other visits" (14). In other words, rather than coming from linear sequence and structure, meaning comes from a discursive pile-up: from the accumulation of discourses or information, from the mixing of different forms of knowledge. This narrative strategy which emphasizes a dialogic structure reflects many similar techniques prefigured by writers like Virginia Woolf, who also recognized that writing about war or writing within the context of war forces one to look at language and representation differently. Lessing's use of a dialogic form shows us a specifically narrative site where meaning collapses or emerges, not according to action and character or the drama of any primary experience of war, but according to the flow of competing discourses.

Like the stories she uses to point to the instability of truth, Lessing uses a variety of stories of the perpetual military organization of society to point to a story of how the military organization of civilian society penetrates the psyche as well. Alongside a story of the successive wars that have merged the power of the military, the arms industry, and science, Lessing produces a second text, a psychic version of geographic war. In the case of *Shikasta*, then, physical places and physical events correspond to structures of consciousness. In other words, truth, as well as the truth of war or military movement have no stable position in the mind, the world or the text.

For example, for Johor, what is particularly different between the memories he has accumulated and the current mission extends from space to consciousness. In memory Johor recalls a visit to a prehistoric period in The Round City populated by two peoples, Giants and Natives. In the past, the two species thrived in a symbiotic relationship. While the Giants were twice the size of the Natives and intellectually superior, the relationship between the two groups was based on a model of tutelary relations:

> The Giants' reason for being, their function, their use, was the development of the Natives, who were their other halves, their own substances. But the Natives had nothing ahead of them but degeneration. . . . The Giants were in the position of the healthy, or healthier twin who will be saved in an operation in which the other one must die. (38)

In this relationship, in which the Giants don't even recognize the word "enemy . . . the word fled by them, unmarked, it did not strike home anywhere" (36), Johor was sent to alert the species that "their history was over" (38). Johor's mission in the past was to look for signs of a psychic disease that attacks the soul and moral structure of a species and leaves them with assumptions of superiority. In addition, his mission included helping people "to identify with [them]selves as individuals" (38).

His current mission to the twentieth century is quite different. The culture he remembered, one in which relationships between people and groups were based on mutual respect and cooperation, a culture that "thrived in peace, mutual help, aspirations for more of the same" (22) has, through a cosmic event, dissolved:

> A particularly arrogant and self-satisfied breed, a minority of the minority white race, dominates most of Shikasta, a multitude of different races, cultures, and religions which, on the whole [are] superior to that of the oppressors. (83)

Thus the main difference between the memory and the present is that in the past the species' inability to comprehend concepts such as "enemy" "individualism," and "superiority" gives way to the present where a culture devotes all its energy to the achievement of superiority and war. But this is no simple ignorance-was-bliss and knowledge-is-our-downfall narrative setup. In this contrast between periods, specific psychic developments correspond to specific technological and political ones. Feelings such as the evolution of "superiority" are connected to a pattern of endless wars in which the power of the military, the production of arms, and advances in science and technology are their own industry, represented as signs of the mental disease Johor was sent to investigate. All forms of reporting—factual, memoirs, case studies, stories, myths, and historical accounts—collectively form both a history of the species *and* a history of their psychic states. It is no longer possible to treat history or war as an event apart from developments in structures of consciousness. One would have to forget one's own psychic being in order to say that war is "out there," and that is precisely what Lessing is pointing out. She disrupts the idea that war happens on the battlefield and connects war to the psychic world, putting the two in dialogic relation to one another. Furthermore, readers must confront the problem that they are, like all of the dialogic forms set up in the novel, in a relationship where one position *interferes* with the other, precluding traditional resolution in favor of suspending narrative possibilities. To tell the "truth" of war Lessing abandons literary tropes such as irony or pastoral remove and replaces them with an investigation of the unstable and discursive nature of reality. Reality only emerges through collective discourse.

Another example of the relation between two "worlds"—psychic and physical—comes in the form of an energy given off by Canopus: the Substance of We Feeling (or SOWF). Recalling a Golden Age myth, SOWF is a physical force which cannot be found on earth, but must be supplied by a greater power beyond earth. Johor records SOWF as a vibration similar to a radio wave received by certain arrangements of buildings, spaces or one's inner self. An "accident of the stars" seriously reduces the SOWF energy for the Shikastans, after which Johor finds them the victims of a confused, aggressive, greedy society. For Johor SOWF is a psycho-somatic force absolutely vital to Shikastans, a "rich and vigorous air, which kept everyone safe and healthy, and above all made them love one another" (73). Johor records that Shikastans experience the reduction in the radiance as emotionally crippling. At the time of Johor's latest visit, Shikastans have no recollec-

War as Narrative Discourse

tion of a time in which there was an abundance of SOWF, and therefore have no perspective from which to understand their chaotic and violent present. At issue for Shikastans, and a goal for Johor, is the recovery of their memories even though they live in a disorienting and chaotic world dominated by military control. Lessing makes that process of recovery a discursive one, one dependent on many voices, documents, and interpretations, none of which ever carry exclusive authority. Recovering memory involves collecting contradictory documents and voices.

To do that requires looking at the narrative options Lessing offers. Earlier I argued that the main narration, Johor's, is incomplete, interrupted, and doubled from part one of the novel to part two. Another dialogic structure is found at the level of protagonists and antagonists. Ordinarily combatants, soldiers and terrorists are mixed up in *Shikasta*. Dislocated from historical or geographic markers, soldiers and terrorists are redefined. Individual psyches that are ordinarily thought of as opposites are forced to wrap around a common understanding of violence to forge identities. For instance, armies are redefined as the answer to civilian unrest:

> It was clear what had to be done. And it was done. Numbers of these potential arsonists and destroyers were taken into various military organizations that had civilian designations; what was done, in fact, was what always was done in times of such disturbances on Shikasta. (233)

Similarly, the terrorists in Lessing's text are defined by their relative success in constituting identities around the central theme of violence in a world in which violence is the organizing power. I say "successfully" because these figures do not fall into psychosis in the face of cultural and psychic fragmentation, but rather recollect their fragmented identities based on the unifying structure of violence. The extreme of such a recollected fragmentation leads to an alternative to the army in a culture saturated by war: a good terrorist. One is reminded of Gibson's remarks about a "New War" and the new combatants of that war. For example, INDIVIDUAL TYPE SIX (Terrorist Type Eight):

> When his group of a dozen young men and women crystallized out finally it was not on the basis of any particular political creed. Everyone had been formed by experiences of emotional or physical deprivation, had been directly affected by war. None could do anything but fix the world with a cold, hating eye: *This is what you are like*. (135)

In other words, selves are made from the ruins of war and economy because they are the strongest ruins left to choose from. Another example of a successful terrorist, or a successful citizen of violence, is INDIVIDUAL SEVEN (Terrorist Type 5), a young woman: "This was a child of rich parents, manufacturers of an internationally known household commodity of no use whatsoever, contributing nothing except to the economic imperative: thou shalt consume" (137). Violence and a multinational, high capitalist drive merge to form a disfigured civilian population. Youth, then, the carriers of the "future," having witnessed "the breakdown of their culture into barbarism" (138), organize, divide and subdivide like cells:

> Thus it came about that in this infinitely subdivided society, where different sets of ideas could exist side by side without affecting each other—or at least not for long periods—the mechanisms like parliaments, councils, political parties, groups championing minority ideas, could remain unexamined, tabooed from examination of a cool rational sort, while in another area of society, psychologists and sociologists could be receiving awards and recognition for work, which were it to be applied, would destroy this structure entirely. (139)

Identities have nowhere to turn but into terrorism because the examination of political activity, along with militarism and technology, "had joined the realm of the sacred—the tabooed"(139). In such a world all human development is invisibly connected to war. Like modern military technology in the late twentieth century, modern military systems of organization in *Shikasta* not only represent ever increasing modes of violence and the ideologies that sustain them (democracy, multinationalism, capitalism), they also paradoxically make invisible what is most visible, that is, the fact that psyches are built out of violent ruins and society is based on war. In addition, by using Johor's shifting point of view Lessing is able to set up a dialogic struture around the question of nationalism as a protective form of social myth and common identity which shields them from enemies "out there" and nationalism as a conquerable evil that can only lead to war. In fact, the only antagonist that emerges in the novel is nationalism with all its discursive forms of substantiation, religious, political, scientific:

> **Politics, political parties, which attract exactly the same emotions as religions did and do, as nations did and do, spawn new creeds every day . . . Everywhere ideas, sets of mind, beliefs that have supported people for centuries are fraying away, dissolving, going. (197)**

Interestingly, this is a theme and a set of formal questions taken up by Kathy Acker in *Empire of the Senseless* as well as Leslie Silko in *Almanac of the Dead* as each exposes the intimate relation between constructions of war, multinationalism, and sexuality. But Lessing isn't so much interested in deconstructing multinationalism as she is in exposing how the *story* of a multinational, violence-saturated society is built, how structures of language and consciousness forge strategies by which cultures rationalize their own violence. Lessing's critique is, above all, a narrative project centered on our *representations* of war and their shattering of cause and effect:

War as Narrative Discourse

Heroisms and escapes and braveries of local and limited kind were raised into national preoccupations, which were in fact forms of religion. But this not only did not assist, but prevented, an understanding of how the fabric of cultures had been attacked and destroyed. After each war, a renewed descent into barbarism was sharply visible—but apparently cause and effect were not connected, in the minds of Shikastans. (89)

We can read how stories of heroism and bravery literally cover our understanding of our explicit role in warfare by scrutinizing the problem with the categories of protagonist and antagonist, categories that find their strongest narrative form in the "hero." Thus, what Johor finds in the future—race wars, barbarism, the politics of superiority—is informed by these very impulses to forget war through stories of "heroism" and "enemies."

Lessing presses in on religion and the structure of belief in the above passage in a way similar to Elaine Scarry's arguments in her book *The Body In Pain: The Making and Unmaking of the World*. Scarry argues that war produces a crisis in belief that abruptly sends a population back to very early stages of understanding itself because the world must quickly be reinvented. In such a crisis ideas that have little or no basis in the material world can "borrow" the physical body in order to substantiate the appearance of reality. According to Scarry, in an activity of "reality conferring," the outcome of war has its substantiation "in a process of perception that allows extreme attributes of the body to be translated into another language, broken away from the body and relocated elsewhere at the very moment that the body itself is disowned, made to disappear" (124).[2] Most pertinent to my discussion, Scarry argues that the material world is distanced from the outcome of war, that is, armies of injured bodies, and relocated on issues and ideas that result in abstract constructions such as winners and losers, heroes and villains, and victims and executioners. In Scarry's terms, Lessing both stages and disturbs the narrative structures by which populations reinvent themselves during the crisis of war, showing us how narrative is both the site of destruction *and* possibility. Terrorist emerges as a plausible identity, heroism is revealed as a coverstory for killing. The emphasis in Lessing's novel is on the specifically discursive process by which a population builds the faith—and the stories that will support it—to keep going in the face of global destruction.

Up until now I have been describing an overall narrative strategy employed by Lessing in different ways in the novel. I have briefly discussed Lessing's disturbance of antagonist/protagonist categories. However, this narrative strategy finds its strongest form in the character of Johor/George. A closer reading of the character of Johor and his particular function in the novel shows us where Lessing has taken the narrative formal features connected to protagonists and their dramatic action. Put simply, George (who is Johor born on Earth in this latest visit), is sent to Earth to subvert the occupation of Europe and North America by the Chinese and to stop a global race war. Perhaps the strongest example of the effect and affect attributable to

George's appearance in the novel happens at "The Trial," a symbolic event orchestrated by the youth armies of the world. The white race is on trial for its centuries of crimes against all dark races. George is from the start a character made up of mixed races, cultures and lineage; he is dark-haired and olive-skinned, raised in North Africa, educated in the West.

According to Lynn Hanley in *Writing War*, the character is meant to be mutable for a reason: "Metaphorically, he is being educated to baffle the categorical impulse, the impulse at the root of our bellicosity to pen human beings within arbitrary, mutually exclusive, and hostile boundaries" (120). The world in which he finds himself is filled with nothing but hostile encounters, and yet his character moves in and out between them with relative ease, partly because Johor exhibits a talent for mutability that other characters do not. At various points in the novel he represents the Islamic Youth Federation for the Care of the Cities, the Jewish Guardians of the Poor, and the United Christian Federation of Young Functionaries for Civil Care. Combine those roles with other characters' descriptions of him, and with his dual presence in parts one and two of the novel, and you have a character who only morphs. Rather than a unified and autonomous main character, George functions as a fictive strategy for interrupting the subject of war. His character works as a transitory figure, an as yet unfinished subject or subject in process that enters and exits history at the very points at which a western metaphysical tradition of the war as agon, or contest model is played out. In addition, he is not laboring to save any one race, but is instead laboring to recollect the memories of relationship that might join warring peoples. Unlike a prot(agon)ist, George stands in for a point of view always mutable, never autonomous, a position from which an alternative to war might emerge through discursive possibilities.

The Trial is represented as an event reminiscent of a contemporary made-for-television movie: the setting is Greece, the birthplace of Western society and culture. Its audience consists for the most part of young, angry, disenfranchised and suspicious members of the warring parties on the planet. Any form of organization of these masses is nearly non-existent. In addition, there is not enough food or water, nor satisfactory accommodations; the members from both Europe and the emergent nations arrive emotionally and physically starved and in a state of poverty; it's too hot, too noisy, filthy and crowded. Resembling a refugee camp, the setting of the trial is characterized as a specifically war-torn chaos.

George, considered by his audience to be a white man, is elected to represent the dark races against the white race. An elderly white English man, John Brent-Oxford, is elected to represent the defense. George's entourage is a group of children from every race, and John Brent-Oxford is always accompanied by George's brother, Benjamin, and one white and one black child. The audience is also mixed, unsegregated by gender, nationality or race, with the exception of the Chinese, "the only national group which was allotted a special position and marked with a banner" (318). The witnesses George calls

War as Narrative Discourse 51

include a Native American, a South American Indian, a Zimbabwean, a Vietnamese. Each tells how the white race, redefined through military and economic power instead of "racial" designation, is responsible for century after century of brutality, ignorance, oppression, torture, colonization and aggression against nonwhite races.

What is remarkable about the trial is not the trial itself, but the dissolving of dramatic or climactic narrative drive. After eight nights of testimony about war crimes, the formal hearings begin to take second place to informal meetings during the breaks in the trial. New relationships are formed, lovers find one another in unforeseen ways across racial and class boundaries, and revenge feelings dissipate. In fact, what is ordinarily the central divisive principle among countless nations and peoples, that is, race, becomes decentralized. The traditional dichotomous models of contention in contemporary culture are dislocated from history. For example, the trial of black against white—the ultimate agon of a culture of bellicosity—peters out, the delegates scatter over the world, and nothing more is heard of the inevitable wiping out of the European populations. This narrative strategy follows a pattern set up in a variety of ways in the novel, that of a dialogic structure in which oppositions are broken down, mixed up, and dissolved rather than resolved.

Along with a fizzling of the victims' and the oppressors' dramatic tension, or agon, the defense disperses its dramatic potential as well when John Brent-Oxford offers only this as an answer, "with no effort to be heard": "I plead guilty to everything that has been said. How can I do anything else?" (335). To which a member of the crowd offers up, lightheartedly, "Well, what are we going to do? Lynch him?" (335). The general reactions range from laughter, to anger, to silence, to confusion as all recognizable "verdicts of history" are, at best, dismissed. The defense's last words? An unsettling counterstance that fails to resolve the problem and yet suspends the possibility of recognizing the contest in oneself:

> I want to ask all of you present: Why is it that you, the accusers, have adopted with such energy and efficiency the ways you have been criticizing . . . Why is it that so many of you who have not been forced into it, have chosen to copy the materialism, the greed, the rapacity of the white man's technological society? (334)

While anger and indignation permeate the camp, two other events conquer the emotions. One, it rains, and two, the heat lessens because of the rain. Many people go to sleep while their anger dissipates "because of the easing of the tension due to the drop in temperature—and due also, to the general feeling of anticlimax." (335).

It is this narrative anticlimax that marks Lessing's final fictive strategy to relocate war. Put simply, the story cannot sustain itself because its protagonist, its antagonist, and its climax are lost. The main arena or environment is displaced, the main conflict dissolves, the main character's voice is supplanted by many voices, the main action is robbed of its dramatic tension, and meaning is dispersed and scattered out across a field of stories, relationships and languages: "Hundreds of conversations between couples, among groups, in 'seminars'" (336) replace the primary speeches and speakers. The "trial" becomes a carnival in which the predominant mode is "laughter" and a "singing" that threatens to drown out the talking, similar to the way that the gathering in Leslie Silko's novel *Almanac of the Dead* disperses and distorts the conflict. The trial takes what ordinarily feeds the story of guilt vs. innocence, that is, the idea of victims and oppressors and the rhetorical structures that support those ideas, and mixes up the figures, actions, and drama. Even the sanctity of guilt and innocence falls away, along with the rhetorical structures that support them, such as defenses of nationalism for the oppressor and defenses of powerlessness for the victim, as George Sherban "counters" traditions with a suggestion of self introspection:

> I want to make a single observation. It is that for three thousand years India has persecuted and ill-treated a part of its own population. I refer to the Untouchables. The unspeakable treatment meted out to these unfortunate people, *barbaric, cruel, senseless* . . . this unspeakably cruel treatment is matched for baseness by nothing the white races have ever done. At this time millions upon millions of people in the subcontinent of India are treated worse than the white oppressor ever treated a black man or woman. This is not a question of a year's oppression, a decade's persecution, a century's ill-treatment, not the results of a short-lived and unsuccessful regime like the British Empire, not a ten-year outburst of savagery like Russian communism, but something built into a religion and a way of life, a culture, so deeply embedded that the frightfulness and ugliness of it apparently cannot even be observed by the people who practice it. (337)

In place of binary oppositions, the cornerstone of language, culture and identity, we find a gap of sorts, a place where guilt and innocence are no longer readable in the same way. Out of this chaotic, parodic and noisy ruin comes an unusual opportunity, the opportunity for a new story that might interrupt the story of war. George's final proposal to the audience is neither an argument projecting guilt or claiming innocence, but rather a new form of self-criticism.

Just as Kathy Acker makes the argument in her novel *Empire of the Senseless* that the hateful eye/I is created by the dominant culture, Lessing seems to be suggesting that one must admit the existence or effects of that hateful eye inside in order to remember that war is the disease we carry within us, a disease that has affected our deepest understandings of ourselves as individuals and as nations or groups. Her novel's climax disrupts a system of "justice" that must project guilt outward to sustain a story of blame as it restores winners and losers to their rightful, warring positions. It does so by deflating the narrative tension and dispersing it back out over a field of pos-

War as Narrative Discourse

sibilities, including suspending "winning" in favor of accepting an as yet unfinished, plural, and mutable discussion, rather than ending in a harsh battle or climax. It is that formal and thematic story-making process, the desire to tell the story of winners and losers, that Lessing criticizes, to the extent that she tries to "catch" the narrative movement at the "place" where she finds war being written—in the narrative structures and social discourses we use to describe ourselves and in the individual and cultural psychic structures that govern us.

In terms of Lessing's narrative, the effects of war are located at the level of narrative structures, social discourse and individual and cultural consciousness. In *Shikasta*, as I have argued, she compares civilian and military communities as well as spatial and psychic settings and exposes their dialogic relation. At the level of narrative structure the stories a culture tells itself about individual and societal identity already stage the potential conditions of war, *as well as* the possibilities available for avoiding war. By looking at how the memory and the place of war are constructed, and by locating war at the level of narrative structures and social discourse, we may begin to read how it is that the war novel in particular relies on *and* undoes the way we talk about war. As contemporary theory has shown us, looking at history in terms of narrative structures and social discourses is already an enterprise taken up by psychoanalysis, poststructuralism and postmodernism. In the study of the novel, we might now begin to ask how we can add to that enterprise specific changes in our understandings of war and representation, an idea I take up in the next chapters.

NOTES

1. Gilbert and Gubar argue that economic decline for women during the years between World War I and World War II generated a whole series of labor opportunities based on war efforts, such as the Women's Auxiliary Corps and the Women's Royal Naval Service. By about 1942 the female labor force in the United States and Britain had increased by over 40%, "approximately three-quarters of it consisting of married women" (213). In other words, war brought with it a certain kind of liberty and opportunity for women, relief from the limits of being a housewife and mother, for instance, and entrance into a form, albeit a form without post-war life, of militarism and politics previously precluded. The works of Virginia Woolf seem to point to many ambiguous areas of freedom/oppression available or enacted upon women during the wars. For instance, the Great War's gender implications of war as a sexual turning point are at work in *Mrs. Dalloway, Jacob's Room*, and *Three Guineas*. Post-World War II writers, including Lessing and H.D., extended these themes toward different ends, and sexuality as a wartime issue certainly was present in feminist documents of the time, such as Mary Austin's "Sex Emancipation Through War" (1918).

2. Scarry goes on to discuss ancient and contemporary examples of why and how the body should, in certain moments of crisis and creation such as war, have

such a power of substantiation, particularly in her analysis of scenes of wounding in the Bible. Particularly pertinent to my study are Scarry's claims that in order to construct belief systems populations rely on the extreme experience of and narrativize war as a method of substantiation. Elaine Pagels traces a different but related cultural production in *The Gnostic Gospels*, particularly in her arguments about good and evil and God the Father and God the Mother.

CHAPTER IV
Nuclear Ideology and Narrative Displacement

Don DeLillo's texts are disturbing, writes one critic, because they reflect the "bloodless" heart of postmodernism, where violence and consumer culture fill the same spiritual void that Nazism—the last authentic evil—filled. In a world that levels all of history and human experience to representation and commodity, even Hitler, the antagonist who ought to serve as the ultimate narrative telos of stories of evil, could become a product of the open market, a routine, an identity dissolved into a sea of possibilities. And that is exactly what happens in Don DeLillo's novel, *White Noise*, bringing us rather quickly to a common postmodern question. If history, the subject, and meaning are all dismantled, what's left at the bloodless heart of postmodernism? In this chapter I will concentrate on showing how several thematic displacements of war occur at the level of narrative structure and strategy. For the remainder of this discussion I will use the term narrative displacement to refer to the shifting of thematic authority to a structural feature or question. Furthermore, I will focus on the foreclosure of modernist narrative options activated by the historical specificity of the literary postmodern.

Many of Don DeLillo's novels carry the theme of war as a kind of background noise that pervades all of contemporary human existence. For instance, Glen Selvy, the undercover soldier in *Running Dog* (1978) and Jack Gladney, narrator of *White Noise* (1985), share a common feature in that each does "battle" with the "deadening" effects of their respective cultures. Similarly, the novel *End Zone* (1986) explores an obsession with self-annihilation and nuclear holocaust, and *Americana* (1989) characterizes the relationship between asceticism and apocalypse as "the purest of deaths" (50). Many critics have identified the way nuclear peril in particular often works in DeLillo's novels as the strongest metaphor available to shake up what appears to be contemporary culture's anesthetized response to war (Osteen 143; Wilcox 348; Cantor 44). *White Noise* shows us a character who is trying

55

56   Allegories of Violence

to overcome his fear of death and annihilation by mastering a set of discourses of authority and revising the story of his life. The novel cannot be situated within modernist war novel categories because its structure reveals a historically specific set of narrative coordinates, as I will argue.

But in order to approach the novel's use of nuclear apocalypse, it first helps to look at the linguistic nature of nuclear war and its connection to the literary postmodern. Jacques Derrida argues in "No Apocalypse, Not Now" that literature has always been part of the generation of nuclear weaponry:

> [Nuclear weaponry is] a phenomenon whose essential feature is that of being *fabulously textual*, through and through. Nuclear weaponry depends, more than any weaponry in the past, it seems upon structures of information and communication, structures of language, including non-vocalizable language, structures of codes and graphic decoding. But the phenomenon is fabulously textual also to the extent that, for the moment, nuclear war has not taken place; one can only talk and write about it. (23)

Thematically, the subject of nuclear war has of course surfaced in many contemporary science fiction novels of the 1980's. For instance, fictive strategies for comprehending the crisis of nuclear war appear in Russell Hoban's *Riddley Walker*, Maggie Gee's *The Burning Book*, Umberto Eco's *The Name of the Rose*, Doris Lessing's *Canopus in Argos* series, Tim O'Brien's *Nuclear Age* and Bernard Malamud's *God's Grace*.[1] These books not only take on nuclear war as a theme, they represent the nuclear as a dominant condition of contemporary society. One narrative crisis common to each of these works concerns interpretation. Specifically, the question of how to address reader response arises, particularly a numbness to the possibility of nuclear apocalypse that has been thoroughly analyzed. For instance, Robert Jay Lifton describes a state of suspended emotion that has characterized the last fifty years in response to World War II in *Indefensible Weapons: The Political and Psychological Case Against Nuclearism* (1982). He claims that a lack of adequate response, or "numbing," to nuclear warfare is produced when we choose avoidance over engagement:

> We would rather avoid looking at events that, by their very nature must change us and our relation to the world. We prefer to hold on to our presuppositions and habits of personal and professional function. And we may well sense that seriously studying such an event means being haunted by it from then on . . . (39)

Thus, we avoid thinking about nuclear warfare in a process of denial. Each of the novels in my study attempts to develop narrative strategies that might adequately meet the unthinkable.

As Brian McHale points out in *Constructing Postmodernism*, nuclear apocalypse constitutes a unique crisis in representation, a crisis of figurative and

Nuclear Ideology and Narrative Displacement

literal apocalypse met by postmodern fiction with a variety of narrative strategies for displacing the concept of nuclear holocaust. The threat of and the representation of nuclear apocalypse is perhaps productive of the quintessential postmodern space because its structure de-emphasizes the theme of war in order to foreground the randomness of representation. For instance, Thomas Pynchon's novel *Gravity's Rainbow* (1973) leaves us with a concluding image of three missiles from three different historical moments all merged into one—one from the last days of World War II, one at the war's end, and one yet to come—a nuclear warhead poised above the roof of a theater filled with an audience. That concluding scene scoops up a whole historic calendar of war and stories about war and conflates them into a single image. Pynchon drives the reader to relocate war as a representational crisis:

> The rhythmic clapping resonates inside these walls, which are hard and glossy as coal: *Come-on! Start-the show! Come-on! Start-the-show!* The screen is a dim page spread before us, white and silent. The film has broken, or a projector bulb has burned out. It was difficult even for us, old fans who've always been at the movies (haven't we?) to tell which before the darkness swept in. The last image was too immediate for any eye to register . . . And in the darkening and awful expanse of screen something has kept on, a film we have not learned to see . . . it is now a closeup of the face, a face we all know— (887)

One can hear the echo in DeLillo's *Running Dog*: "That whole bunch, they were movie-mad" (237).

Postmodernist fiction has thus developed a range of narrative strategies for displacing the nuclear. According to McHale, three narrative strategies in particular characterize the postmodern novel's response to war. Nuclear apocalypse may be displaced onto some other apocalypse scenario, as in the case of *Gravity's Rainbow*, as well as Hoban's *Riddley Walker*. Secondly, nuclear apocalypse may be displaced onto the fantastic mode, including the development of other worlds characteristic of science fiction, such as Doris Lessing's *Canopus in Argos* series or Maggie Gee's *The Burning Book*. Lastly, the displacement of nuclear apocalypse may happen at the level of narrative itself, "both as a realistic consequence of nuclear destruction visited on the culture of which this language is a vehicle, and as a kind of text-length metaphor of apocalypse" (161). In this last strategy, language is "pulverized, fused, ruined, reconfigured" (161). I would like to extend McHale's definitions of displacement by arguing the same model in specifically literary terms. That is, by pitting modernism against postmodernism, *White Noise* displaces nuclear apocalypse onto specifically narrative structures such as the construct of the male hero, the promise of purity and epiphany available through crisis, the narrative trajectory informed by the oedipal model, and death as a narrative telos.

On its surface, *White Noise* is a novel about a world in which a reified, mediaspeak "white noise" has replaced coherent meaning. The main character, Jack Gladney, and his "nuclear" family are stuck in a sea of surplus data and electronic waves that saturate their society. For Jack, the white-noise world borders on the apocalyptic. In this setting he searches for something to hold on to if meaning is no longer possible. As Jack asks himself and his world how to negotiate a nostalgic desire for the past with an apocalyptic and incoherent experience of the present, the reader finds narrativized the difference between the modernist world and the postmodern one. Jack Gladney is a modernist displaced in a postmodern world. When he hears his daughter Steffie whispering the words "Toyota Corolla, Toyaota Celica, Toyota Cressida" in her sleep, he responds: "Whatever its source, the utterance struck me with the impact of a moment of splendid transcendence" (155). Against postmodern odds Jack tries over and over again to find a moment of transcendent meaning in his simulation-saturated world.

The novel's structure reflects this theme in three sections that stage three different attempts Jack makes to understand his world: "Waves and Radiation," "The Airborne Toxic Event," and "Dylarama." Each section represents a series of incomprehensible experiences which result in a kind of apocalyptic vision, a kind of death for, respectively, the family, the culture, and an individual. In McHale's terms, *White Noise* is organized structurally and thematically around displacing nuclear destruction by presenting the reader with three versions of war and death, first through technology's atomization of the family, then through a simulacral toxic shock in which the real is displaced by simulation, and finally with the individual's inability to distinguish between the obsession with and fear of "real" death vs. representational death. The central structure of the novel is narrative displacement. In addition, each section has a random quality; they are not chronologically ordered, they follow no necessary cause/effect pattern, and they are and are not dependent on one another for meaning.

Clearly one of the disturbing things about reading DeLillo's novel is the random combination of narrative features. Images that seem to have nothing to do with the story rush by, such as The Most Photographed Barn in America. Commercial slogans tumble out of the mouth of Jack's daughter and occur to him in moments without meaning. B-movie scenes direct Jack's actions, as when he is inexplicably compelled to shoot Willy Mink in the end of the novel. Hack detective novel scenes also play themselves out when Jack has a "showdown" with Mink in a dark office. Historically significant people and events such as Hitler and World War II continually lose their value through bad jokes and commercial trading. While this flurry of narrative features helps to propel the novel, it also erects a wall of static where readers meet the failure of meaning, a paralysis of sorts in which "meaning" itself is set sailing. But an even more disturbing feature of the novel is the site to which the accumulation of narrative features leads us, a site where Hitler and Elvis, the hypnotic power of a totalitarian dictator and the hypnotic blur of drugs, music, rock stars, and television, the most photographed barn in

Nuclear Ideology and Narrative Displacement 59

America and the Airborne Toxic Event are all conflated. If the displacements and conflations are meant to build something readable, what is it? If reality is under attack by simulacral invasion, how do we read it? And is it fair to call that attack a representational war?

One of the guiding metaphors in DeLillo's novel is history as supermarket. In DeLillo's history, even Hitler is a commodity. The novel proceeds to devalue, commodify, and sell Hitler in high capitalist fashion through Jack Gladney's academic subculture. Like the departments of a supermarket, Gladney arranges Hitler in an academic department of Hitler Studies. As Paul Cantor puts it in "Adolph, We Hardly Knew You," "Once a horrifying phenomenon like Hitler can be represented, it can be stripped of its aura and turned into a commodity" (44).

"There is no Hitler building as such," remarks Jack Gladney, only "a dark brick structure we share with the popular culture department, known officially as American environments" (9). From the beginning Hitler as a proper name is reduced to a supermarket-style legacy. Academic disciplines are represented as "departments" that feature history as a set of products: "We are quartered in Centenary Hall, a dark brick structure we share with the popular culture department" (9). Hitler is one in a series of commodities available in an open academic market:

> You've established a wonderful thing here with Hitler. You created it, you imagined it, you nurtured it, you made it your own. Nobody on the faculty of any college or university in this part of the country can so much as utter the word Hitler without a nod in your direction, literally or metaphorically. This is the center, the unquestioned source. He is now your Hitler, Gladney's Hitler. (11)

However, Hitler the commodity has lost its power as a sign of supreme historical value; according to DeLillo, he doesn't even have his own building because in late twentieth-century capitalism he can be endlessly represented and commodified. This information necessarily begs the question, what happened to the narrative power of war and Hitler to provide a meaningful narrative telos for the story?

In his reading of *White Noise* Cantor makes an intriguing connection between Nazism and postmodernism by claiming that the way Hitler restored meaning to people who had lost their traditional bearings is connected to our own moment; we too have lost our bearings in a world saturated by violence, we too are mesmerized by the aesthetic spectacle presented to us via television, and we too search for ways to restore meaning in such a disorienting time. We find partial salvation in the late twentieth-century in the power of consumer-culture and through advanced media and communications technologies. Jack Gladney speaks in precisely these terms: "The world is full of abandoned meanings"(184), which he finds in gadgets, slogans, and technological objects such as computers, garbage disposals, and ATM machines. It is as if Jack is lost in a world of lost meanings, and in such a world Hitler looks attractive as a buyable commodity because he has, at the very least, staying power, charisma of a sort, a "restorative" power—if by restorative we mean something extreme to care about when nothing much matters.

Add to this equation the fact that Jack's job as "the most prominent figure in Hitler studies in North America" is accompanied by the fact that he speaks no German: "I could not speak or read it, could not understand the spoken word or begin to put the simplest sentence on paper" (31). This produces a classic postmodern set up: Hitler's value and the war surrounding Hitler have so depreciated that they are useful commodities for academic scam artists. In other words, Jack is a false authority of "Hitler Studies." He is more accurately described as a salesman, in that he is trying to sell his area of specialization to his department. The best Hitler can achieve in an open market is a trade-show-like appearance as a topic for an academic conference:

> He asked me why I'd chosen this year in particular to learn German, after so many years of slipping past the radar. I told him there was a Hitler conference scheduled for next spring at the College-on-the-Hill. Three days of lectures, workshops, and panels. Hitler scholars from seventeen states and nine foreign countries. Actual Germans would be in attendance. (33)

I agree in part with Cantor's observation that the novel portrays the use and abuse of Hitler as a commodity, but he also claims that consumer culture and Nazi Germany are untroubled parallel worlds in this novel. I would argue that the parallel worlds are set up the way they are in this novel in order to emphasize narrative structures, perhaps relentlessly so. That is, what interrupts the conflation of Nazism and consumer culture happens at the level of narrative form and historical specificity. *White Noise* is above all else site specific, even as its displacements challenge interpretation. The mall, the supermarket, the particular forms of academia emerging from the novel are each specific to late twentieth century America. Modernism and Nazi Germany must be in dialogue with postmodernism and consumer culture not because they have a chronological, essential relationship, but *because their relationship is bound to narrative structures,* as I will argue.

Consumerism offers another kind of narrative exchange in the aura of family connectedness that Jack finds at the shopping mall in two ways. First, in place of kinship, shopping now connects the family, with the structure of family rooted in economic consumption: "My family gloried in the event. I was one of them, shopping at last" (83). In shopping the family finds its glue and Jack finds a transitional identity:

> We moved from store to store . . . There was always another store, three floors, eight floors, basement full of cheese graters and paring knives. I shopped with reckless abandon. I shopped for immediate needs and distant contingencies. I shopped for its own sake, looking and touching, inspecting

Nuclear Ideology and Narrative Displacement 61

merchandise I had no intention of buying, then buying it . . . I filled myself out, found new aspects of myself, located a person I'd forgotten existed. Brightness settled around me. (84)

Beyond this scene's metaphoric value, or, shopping as family tie, it parodies the modernist novel's heroic moment of vision structures Jack as a subject, since he "finds himself" in this setting. There is a difference between the modernist protagonist's anxiety and the strategies to overcome it, on the one hand, and the postmodernist subject's inability to deploy the same strategies for overcoming the chaos of the world, on the other. The modernist novel's protagonist can be described in general as an autonomous individual confronted with chaos, an individual who experiences a transcendent moment of vision—or epiphany—that guides him to an awareness of either the lost order of a past world, or an internal self, a private sphere wherein he finds meaning. This is exemplified by books such as Richard Ellmann and Charles Feidelson's *The Modern Tradition: Backgrounds of Modern Literature* (1965), Irving Howe's *The Idea of the Modern in Literature and the Arts* (1967) and Lionel Trilling's *Beyond Culture* (1968). For example, in Joyce's *Portrait of the Artist as a Young Man*, the main character Stephen experiences a climactic revelation at the sight of a young woman wading on the shore of the ocean. Or, in Woolf's *To The Lighthouse*, as in many of her novels, stream of consciousness narration is used to convert the story of outer action and events into a story of the life of the mind. The protagonist thus finds meaning in an "inner world" unavailable in the world collapsing around her. In contrast, in the previous example, Jack Gladney's moment of vision is based on a superficial and ridiculous parody of an epiphany. His grand moment of vision happens in a dizzy whir of products offered to him through the experience of high-powered shopping.

Secondly, shopping malls are not only a sign of our times, they are historic markers that show us how our connectedness to meaning is changing. The interpretation of this scene depends on an understanding of the shopping mall as a particular, late twentieth-century, capitalist invention, producing a particular, twentieth-century subject. This scene is projected not as a description of action, but rather as an arresting of narrative movement in which the character is fixed by his setting, a setting characterized by images and signs that engulf reality and subjects:

People swarmed through the boutiques and gourmet shops. Organ music rose from the great court. We smelled chocolate, popcorn, cologne; we smelled rugs and furs, hanging salamis and deathly vinyl. My family gloried in the event . . . I filled myself out, found new aspects of myself, located a person I'd forgotten existed. (83-84)

Fredric Jameson charts the disappearance of familiar modernist and realist conventions in contemporary art in his book *Postmodernism, or, the*

Cultural Logic of Late Capitalism. In a by now central analysis of postmodernity, he argues that the alienation of the subject characteristic of modernism and associated with Freud is being displaced by the subject's fragmentation, a phenomenon particular to postmodernity and late capitalism, with questions of representation linked to shifts in subjectivity. As Jameson describes the stakes, postmodernity is a periodizing concept that gives us a way to understand subjectivity and representation as they are inscribed by economy:

> The end of the bourgeois ego, or monad, no doubt brings with it the end of the psychopathologies of that ego. . . . But it means the end of much more—the end, for example, of style, in the sense of the unique and the personal, the end of the distinctive . . . As for expression and feelings or emotions, the liberation, in contemporary society, from the older anomie of the centered subject may also mean not merely a liberation from anxiety but a liberation from every other kind of feeling as well, since there is no longer a self present to do the feeling. This is not to say that the cultural products of the postmodern are utterly devoid of feeling, but rather that such feelings—which it may be better and more accurate, following J. F. Lyotard, to call "intensities,"—are now free-floating and impersonal and tend to be dominated by a peculiar kind of euphoria . . . "(16)

The markers of late capitalism include media-scapes, shopping malls, advanced technology of all kinds, information highways. In Jameson's terms, alienated subjects like Jack in *White Noise* become free-floating intensities. Jack is on the verge of becoming the quintessentially postmodern character; or, more precisely, Jack's character is dissolving into the language of the text. In place of a developed psychology we get a free-floating one, one that is subject to the "euphoria" of consumer culture and information technology.

Contemporary views of the literary postmodern trace an identical "delirium" and euphoric experience wherein the subject experiences an undifferentiated flux of pure signifiers, and ecstasy of communication in which traditional structures of meaning dissolve and the ability to imagine an alternative reality disappears (Wilcox 348–49). In this context DeLillo's novel shares a remarkable similarity with Baudrillard's claims in "The Ecstasy of Communication" about the space of postmodern communication, where information devours its own contents. According to Baudrillard, subjects are overstimulated by simulations or "simulacra", an overwhelming cacaphony of media and information culture. When Jack is confronted by commercial slogans or television images, for example, he is brought to a state of euphoria: "Whatever its source . . . it struck me with the impact of a moment of splendid transcendence" (155). Against postmodern odds Jack tries over and over again to find transcendant meaning in his simulation-saturated world.

Instead of meaning coming from narrative development or the rendering of psychological depth of a character through action, a combination of disjunctive scenes "arrests" the narrative in its tracks. In the case of *White*

Nuclear Ideology and Narrative Displacement 63

Noise this happens thematically and structurally—the story is about a man who cannot collect and organize his experiences, and the novel is built out of random narrative structures that stutter and scatter. No longer can we ask, where is the narrative taking the character and the reader (to the mall?). We must ask, how can we put these pieces of narrative together, how can we read, *what is reading*. One could argue that we ask similar questions of Woolf and Joyce. However, in DeLillo's novel, Jack both engages modernist themes and finds that his contemporary postmodern world has obliterated them at the same time. The difference between this character lost in his world and a modernist character lost in his is this: Jack's shopping scene points to *itself* and to the *distance* it has from a scenario in which a character, through chaos and confusion, finds himself and deeper meanings—a modernist character's trajectory. Instead, Jack floats free in a sea of consumer-culture waves:

> A band played live Muzak. Voices rose ten stories from the gardens and promenades, a roar that echoed and swirled through the vast gallery, mixing with noises from the tiers, with shuffling feet and chiming bells, the hum of escalators, the sound of people eating, the human buzz of some vivid and happy transaction. (84)

Thus, shopping delirium is an example of a condition in which a postmodern subject finds themself engulfed by the repetitious images and signs of a twentieth-century consumer-culture overload. Or, put slightly differently, the shopping mall, like the Hitler Studies department, is an example of the narrative distance that the literary postmodern present moment has moved from the literary modernist past.

Part of the evidence for a historical specificity to postmodern narrative strategies is the character of Jack Gladney himself. For example, unlike the protagonist of the modernist novel, an autonomous self capable of discovering a coherent private interior, Jack's "I" wavers like a television wave. In the first section of the novel, "Waves and Radiation," where we meet Jack, we find disconnected chapters that read like random narrative fragments. As Frank Lentricchia argues in "Tales of the Electronic Tribe," "There really is a story (in Jack's) life, but he exerts no authorial control over it." Here we have an "I" narrator who can't find himself, or perhaps more precisely, can't fix itself in the story, in language, in history.

In order to set that "I" in motion DeLillo portrays free floating identity in a scene where Jack and his wife Babette consider a smorgasbord of sexual roles:

> I said, "Pick your century. Do you want to read about Etruscan slave girls, Georgian rakes? I think we have some literature on flagellation brothels. What about the Middle Ages? We have incubi and succubi. Nuns galore." (29)

In the face of the possibility to "be all that you can be" anywhere in history, Jack chooses twentieth-century trashy porn magazines containing smutty letters:

> There is a double fantasy at work in such letters. People write down imagined episodes and then see them published in a national magazine. Which is the greater stimulation? (30)

To which the answer is, it doesn't matter, in a world made up of brand names, advertising slogans, and communication overload. In Baudrillard's terms, there is no inner self; the end of interiority is replaced by a free-floating subjectivity which underlies the experience of the self in the space of simulacrum, a space where the simulation precedes, even blocks the reality it is supposed to represent. Throughout the novel Jack is interrupted by consumer-culture slogans that pepper his thinking: "Mastercard, Visa, American Express" (100); "Leaded, unleaded, superunleaded" (199); "Dristan Ultra, Dristan Ultra" (167).

Jack is no more fixed in the role of father. As the authority of the traditional, nuclear family, Jack continually slips out of his position. Family genealogy amounts to flashes of trivia. For instance, the parents of this family are divorcees arriving with two kids apiece from previous marriages. Who's who is never quite explained; blood lineage is de-emphasized and random constellations form ever-changing orbits. This is not just a clever way to parody the myth of the nuclear family and the authority of paternal lineage. By taking blood ties out of the thematic equation, DeLillo also points to shifts that would necessarily follow in the formal structure of the novel. For at the heart of the narrative impact of the chopped-up family are the corresponding chopped up myths of patriarchy and the oedipal mother-loving (or hating) family, animated for example in Faulkner's novels. In DeLillo's assemblage each of those categories comes apart and is reconstituted in very specific ways. For instance, Jack's family is dispersed into ex-wives and children who travel back and forth between families. When one of Jack's ex-wives contacts him, it is a telephonic relationship: "We greet each other here" (273), she says. His response: "her tiny piping voice bounced down to me from a hollow ball in geosynchronous orbit" (273). Thus the emphasis placed on the blood ties of the family and on masculine authority is displaced onto the primacy of electronic communication.

There are many bankrupt epiphanies in *White Noise* revolving around Jack, but none more poignant than when Jack confronts identity dissolution head-on through the image of Babette's magnified TV face. From early on in the novel Jack represents his wife Babette as his comforting counterpart: "a full-souled woman, a lover of daylight and dense life, the miscellaneous swarming air of families" (5–6). For Jack, Babette is the earth-mother-other, the love he can wrap his identity around, an identity "secure enough to allow itself to be placed in another's care" (29)—or so he wishes her to be. Jack

Nuclear Ideology and Narrative Displacement 65

looks to Babette in order to see a stable version of family, love, self. Several examples in the novel point to TV's all powerful force that threatens to stand in for "the ties that no longer bind." One of the most powerful versions of this is when the family is surprised one night when Babette shows up on TV:

> The face on the screen was Babette's. Out of our mouths came a silence as wary and deep as an animal growl. Confusion, fear, astonishment spilled from our faces. What did it mean? What was she doing there, in black and white, framed in formal borders? Was she dead, missing, disembodied? Was this her spirit, her secret self, some two-dimensional facsimile released by the power of technology, set free to glide through wavebands, through energy levels, pausing to say good-bye to us from the fluorescent screen?.. If she was not dead, was I? a two-syllable infantile cry, ba-ba, issued from the deeps of my soul. (104)

In a moment of dangerous identity crisis Jack is torn away from his Earth-mother vision of Babette and confronted with a simulacral Babette. What Jack sees on the television overwhelms his reality. Jack, his family, his identity, are all reduced to a televised, ghostly death's head. At this moment Jack feels a sudden flash of "strangeness," a "sense of psychic disorientation" (104). His first question is, "If she was not dead, was I?" At such moments Jack loses his identifying space; his ego has nothing to constitute itself against except "a walker in the mists of the dead" (104), a gray image on a screen. In other words, the modernist moment of epiphany is replaced with negative realization and psychic disorientation.

The TV Babette throws his world back out into orbit. Babette is no longer available as the counter-figure against which male identity constitutes itself; in other words, she no longer sustains the oedipal plot trajectory reflected in Jack's claims that "all plots move bedward," toward romance and the heroic achievement of winning love through battle. Babette is a figure in flux, in between things, wave-like. Jack's authority is infantilized, reflected in the cry of an infant. While Jack admits that Babette "comes into full being" there, from his side of the TV screen there is a "mysterious separation"(105) that he tries not to think of as the "journey out of life or death," which it feels like to him. At stake for Jack is how to read Babette so that he can understand himself.

By constructing Babette as a possible threshold of identity, an identity that is provisional and transitional, this scene tells us something about the shift from an alienated, autonomous subject characteristic of modernism toward a fragmented, transitional subject characteristic of postmodernism. Babette's image is one whose primacy destroys myths tied to the real—narrative conventions surrounding domesticity and motherhood, for example, as well as thematic telos focused on heroic epiphanies that provide vision and insight. In effect the scene points to the distance between the desire or nostalgia for a certain story of subjectivity that produced unified individuals and families, and our own, postmodern moment of airwave life. So it is not that the past offered a more authentic experience. And it is not the case that television—and by extension, technology—is evil. And it is not the case that TV Babette is in danger of losing her self. The present distortion shows us how the past was itself a nostalgic construction.

This is no small matter when one remembers that Babette, at least as a traditional feminine figure, is connected to narrative conventions of domesticity, family and love. By crossing the substance/illusion or real/representational boundary, Babette's image provides an almost religious experience for her viewing family. A common reading of this scene points to the way Babette and her image merge, the way "it was but wasn't her," and quickly restores meaning by attaching a moral judgment about the danger of television. But surely we have moved beyond the call to "kill your TV." The other side of the "television is evil and we are all hoodwinked" reading is that maybe that conflation, flesh=image, can tell us something about the *possibilities* of such an indifferentiated moment, rather than just the dangers. Part of the reason the TV Babette mesmerizes the family is that technology has confused the sign with the referent so completely that skin and airwaves blend in a swarm of moving particles. Along with them, conventions surrounding motherhood, the family, and domesticity as narrative trajectories are also obliterated. What if motherhood, the family and domesticity were dislocated, fragmented, scattered back out into the war zone of culture? What would that mean for narrative, for reading, for human subjectivity?

To answer those questions Babette must be read as a crisis in narrative. The trouble for Jack is that Babette keeps slipping out of his idea of her and popping up in the world of postmodern information and media simulacra. Babette puts it best when she describes herself: "[T]he faster a person is moving, the more likely she is to receive only partial hits, glancing rays, deflections" (264). Her provisional subjectivity "deflects" the "hits" and "rays" of Jack's attempts at identity constitution. As a figure of continual forgetting and deferral, accidental action (her seduction), and deflective speed, Babette represents a potential identifying space within which Jack cannot find his reflection. She reduces all his quest-for-meaning yearnings to media babble: "There's enough talk. What is talk? . . . Talk is radio" (264). She reduces his deepest angst to ego-centric childishness: "What is need? We all need. Where is the uniqueness in that" (263)? Jack may construct Babette as the oedipal narrative's mother/other/object of desire, but she falls out of each sign. Neither mother, other, nor object of desire, because she is always "either/or," Babette stands in for the tension between past and present, modernist and postmodernist, real and representational. It is interesting and disturbing to me that so many critics decide to read Babette through Jack without troubling that vision, especially since the novel goes to great lengths to do so.

There hangs Babette, suspended in a static image. Loving mother or monstrous technological ghost? There hangs Jack, wavering between intellectual meaning-hunter and boob-tube head. Which Babette, which Jack do

Nuclear Ideology and Narrative Displacement   67

we want them to be? The question is one of reference. Babette might be read as problematizing the act of reference, as Craig Owens argues about postmodernism in *Beyond Recognition:*

> Postmodernism neither brackets nor suspends the referent but works instead to problematize the activity of reference. When the postmodernist work speaks of itself, it is no longer to proclaim its autonomy, its self-sufficiency, its transcendence; rather, it is to narrate its own contingency, insufficiency, lack of transcendence. It tells of a desire that must be perpetually frustrated, an ambition that must be perpetually deferred; as such, its deconstructive thrust is aimed not only against the contemporary myths that furnish its subject matter, but also against the symbolic, totalizing impulse which characterizes modernist art. (85)

In other words, the question of the nature of evil in the form of technology takes a back seat to developing a resistance to the totalizing impulse of modernist art and its corresponding epistemologies (heroic moments of vision), symbolic authority (the name of the father), and narrative conventions (the oedipal family, death). This nuclear family has been atomized, by the television, the shopping mall, and a world of simulacra, and with it the narrative conventions that sustained it.

The nuclear family's demise and the wavering subjectivity of Jack keep making a strange relay back to war and aestheticization. For example, Thomas Ferarro argues in "Whole Families Shopping at Night" that the television unites us into a fascism, a family fascism, if you will, in which the primacy of the image provides a communal experience that stands in for real human relationships. And indeed it would be easy to support this notion with a reading of *White Noise.* In Ferarro's argument, television threatens to build fascism by giving its viewers something to believe in, by mesmerizing them the same way that Hitler used film to aestheticize violence. Fascism rendered violence aesthetic by translating it into pleasure. One might argue that our attraction or addiction to Peter Jennings delivering the news or our obsession with the O. J. Simpson trial are prime examples of how violence can be rendered aesthetically pleasing. In this reading, the awe the family experiences watching Babette on TV translates into a blind allegiance to a false, politicized image that covers over a violence—in this case, the violence of making the distinction between the real and the representational fuzzy. The connection to "war" is representational.

In *White Noise*, Jack's friend Murray echoes this sentiment in pure postmodern parody:

> I don't trust anybody's nostalgia but my own . . . The more powerful the nostalgia, the closer you come to violence. War is the form nostalgia takes when men are hard-pressed to say something good about their country. (258)

Jack, on the other hand, seems almost addicted to an "aestheticizing habit," as Frank Lentricchia calls it. Jack aestheticizes all of technology, transferring the same mass appeal of fascist tyranny to a lecture about Hitler to his own period's cultural dictator, technology. For Jack, the objects specific to his technological moment, such as the television, provide the communal experience of the image lacking in actual relationships. Even the refrigerator generates an image of beauty and nostalgia: "An eerie static, insistent but near subliminal, that made me think of wintering souls, some form of dormant life approaching the threshold of perception" (258). Jack's nostalgia is precisely the type Murry warns against, the kind that brings one "closer . . . to violence." Murray would say that Jack's extreme nostalgia is tantamount to war, his nostalgia and aestheticization of technology, violence.

Whether or not Jack's repeated attempts to render technology beautiful actually constitute "war," the novel goes on to a second version of war in Section II of *White Noise*, "The Airborn Toxic Event." Section II stages a narrative displacement of nuclear disaster. Not unlike the persona of Hitler, nuclear disaster, once a horrifying phenomenon, is stripped of its aura and turned into a fuzzy blur visible from the backyard:

"The radio calls it a feathery plume," he said. "But it's not a plume."
"What is it?"
"Like a shapeless growing thing. A dark black breathing thing of smoke. Why do they call it a plume?"
"Air time is valuable. They can't go into long tortured descriptions. Have they said what kind of chemical it is?"
"It's called Nyodene Derivative or Nyodene D. It was in a movie we saw in school on toxic wastes. These videotaped rats." (111)

This passage recalls McHale's argument in *Constructing Post-modernism* that postmodernism has developed several narrative strategies for displacing nuclear apocalypse, the central post WWII anxiety, including the displacement of nuclear holocaust onto some other apocalypse scenario, displacement onto other places and times in a kind of "fantastic" realm, and displacement of nuclear apocalypse into the very language of the text itself. *White Noise* borrows a bit from all of these strategies, because the novel is not nuclear war fiction per se, and yet, the nuclear catastrophe is a haunting presence. Defamiliarized into a chemical spill just over the horizon, and connected to its cousin the nuclear family already atomized, the Airborn Toxic event works as a metaphor for nuclear anxiety in the postmodern age.

Susan Sontag has claimed that representations of nuclear war are themselves displacements because every image of collective death is only a kind of metaphor for personal death. In this sense the Airborn Toxic event might stand in for personal death. What is interesting in *White Noise* are the ways in which the metaphors of television and death permeate every sphere of human existence. The Airborn Toxic event merges representation, history

Nuclear Ideology and Narrative Displacement 69

and death through the medium of Jack Gladney who is himself part television camera, part literary recorder:

> The men in Mylex suits moved with lunar caution. Each step was the exercise of some anxiety not provided for by instinct. Fire and explosion were not the inherent dangers here. This death would penetrate, seep into the genes, show itself in bodies not yet born. (116)

Not for nothing does this section follow "Waves and Radiation," in which a family is pulverized by TV waves. The "death" that permeates the first section is one characterized by disjunctive combinations that deconstruct the family. The death in the second section is displaced onto a chemical disaster, representative of a post Cold War nuclear anxiety that is mellowing. The death displaced in section III, entitled "Dylorama," concerns a psychic obsession through drugs and consumer culture. In other words, each section shows us a different angle on the same image: provisional death, as yet unfinished death. To take away the power of death as ontological endpoint is to make death an "ontological pluralizer," as Brian McHale calls it.

McHale argues that television does function quite specifically in *White Noise* as ontological pluralizer, and argues further that television is an allegory for the world of the novel. By that he means that the structure of the fictional world parallels the structure of television itself. The section "Waves and Radiation" keys us in to the features of the structure of televised communication (waves) and nuclear fall-out (radiation), the structure of the world in which Jack, Babette, and their almost-children find themselves free-floating. McHale labels this use of television as *"mise-en-abyme,* or a reduced scale-model of ontological plurality itself" (1992; 130). My own analysis interrupts the conflation McHale makes when he says that TV and death are "routinely equated" in *White Noise* by suggesting there is a gap between television and death, a distance represented by the primacy of the technological image:

> I didn't say it. The computer did. The whole system says it. It's what we call a massive data-base tally. Gladney, J.A.K. I punch in the name, the substance, the exposure time and then I tap into your computer history. Your genetics, your personals, your medicals, your psychologicals, your police-and-hospitals. It comes back pulsing stars. This doesn't mean anything is going to happen to you as such, at least not today or tomorrow. It just means you are the sum total of your data. (141)

The televised Babette can be compared to computer Jack. As Jack and his doctor conclude, "it is real," *because* it is technologically mediated. The massive data-base tally is biologically infected. The computer shows a virus. One thinks of Donna Haraway's description in "The Biopolitics of Postmodern Bodies" of the change from the hierarchical and organic body to the contemporary understanding of the body within recent medical discourse as a coded text, organized as an engineered communications system, ordered by a fluid and dispersed command-control-intelligence network (the immune system). The postmodern body and the postmodern self are fragmented and mediated by and through technology. DeLillo resists placing a true value on these images. His narrative represents them as "data," readable yet undecipherable, present yet opaque, the distancing effects of earlier discourses that gave us whole, organic, unified autonomous bodies and selves.

Thus the "deaths" represented in *White Noise* are both "real" and not. Untethered from its spot in a binary opposition, death hovers as a narrative effect in danger of being replaced by its slicker, more interesting representations. The body turns into a simulation whose effects are recorded by machines, and death loses a great deal of its existential intensity. For example, a practice evacuation complete with SIMUVAC vehicles and men in Mylex suits produces "half an hour of self-induced gagging and vomiting," and the episode is "recorded on videotape and sent somewhere for analysis" (270). Meanwhile, three days later, the actual event carries little weight. An actual noxious odor drifted across the river, causing only a slight sting in the nostril, a watering of the eyes, mostly denial and slightly slower traffic. The final culmination: "About three hours after we'd first become aware of it, the vapor suddenly lifted, saving us from our formal deliberations" (271). In other words, formal deliberations are the best people can muster in the face of the event. The simulated accident has much higher ratings, and real effects. As if to underscore the distance between parallel worlds, Jack discovers that the SIMUVAC figures are using the real event to rehearse and improve a simulation:

> You have to make allowances for the fact that everything we see tonight is real . . . we don't have the victims laid out where we'd want them if this was an actual simulation. (139)

In addition, understandings of death no longer follow a cause and effect pattern:

> Routine things can be deadly, Vern, carried to extremes. I have a friend who says that's why people take vacations. Not to relax or find excitement or to see new places. To escape the death that exists in routine things. (248)

Even when Jack is infected after exposure to the deadly gas Nyodene D, his death is still simulated, an afterimage of a computer scan. Death has been reduced to daily, mundane, routine things, and paranoia has taken hold. Horrific death, like Hitler, barely makes your eyes water. To regain the aura of horrific death one would have to reinvest death with power. And that is exactly what Jack tries to do. For what we find is a choice between the mundane death characteristic of everyday postmodern life, and a return to a distorted nostalgia for horrific death. In fact, the novel constructs a *longing* for, and in the case of Jack's character, a nostalgia for, horrific death.

It is interesting to stop here and note the lengths to which DeLillo goes in order to dislocate and revise death as a narrative convention of the postmodern novel. In order to deconstruct death as a narrative convention, DeLillo must make death into setting, style and character. The ending actions are driven not so much by Jack, but more by the pressure that two periods, two philosophies, two structures have on one another, as if to say modernism cannot leave postmodernism alive, postmodernism cannot leave modernism alive. This is a strange place for the reader to find herself. Is it true that "to plot is to die," as Jack says, or that "to plot is to live," as Murray says, keeping in mind that "to plot" in their discussion is "to plan a killing," and simultaneously, "to make stories?" And what is postmodern narrative, if plot no longer means what narrative strategies *used* to mean: "to plot, to take aim at something, to shape time and space. . . This is how we advance the art of human consciousness" (292)?

The scene in which Jack plots to kill Mink, the man responsible for seducing Babette and delivering Dylar, is almost a mini-novel within the novel. Infected with the phrase, "this was my plan," Jack, driven by sentences and the plot he has going on in his head, is moved to shoot Mink. The end of the heroic narrative is a scene from a detective movie; the great modernism/postmodernism debate has been reduced to TV drama. But it is incorrect to propose, as some critics do, that Jack is a self-fashioned hero whose existence is grounded in nothingness and who is driven by instinct. In truth, Jack is driven by phrases and plots from TV, art, discussions with Murray—in short, by representation itself in all its sacred and profane forms. The unmediated rush of pure experience that Jack *thinks* he is experiencing is really an effect of a beautifully choreographed movie scene, technicolor, sensurround, THX:

> I knew the precise nature of events. I was moving closer to things in their actual state as I approached violence, a smashing intensity. Water fell in drops, surfaces gleamed. (305)

As Leornard Wilcox argues in "Baudrillard, DeLillo's *White Noise*, and the End of the Heroic Narrative," the scene "involves a play of stylistic mannerisms, from the high modernist heroics of the existential hero to the B-movie heroics of the hard-boiled detective" (348).

What is being written is the gap between the seemingly secure narrative position of the heroic figure and, in Baudrillardian terms, the postmodern dispersal of consciousness into screens and networks. When Jack claims, "I knew who I was in the network of meanings" (312), we see his confrontation with Mink as a version of postmodern culture itself. Mink is the postmodern man to excess, the monster vision of a runaway technology with a human head: "His face appeared at the end of the white room, a white buzz" (312) the biological, dark mutant living inside *White Noise*. Jack too experiences the postmodern blitz and stun of surfaces and signifiers. Here the boundaries of self dissolve into the networks and white noise of techno-culture as words become more important than action and flesh:

> I was ready to kill him now. But I didn't want to compromise the plan. The plan was elaborate. Drive past the scene several times, approach the motel on foot, swivel my head to look peripherally into rooms, locate Mr. Gray under his real name, enter unannounced, gain his confidence, advance gradually, reduce him to trembling, wait for an unguarded moment, take out the .25-caliber Zumwalt automatic, fire three bullets into his viscera for maximum slowness, depth and intensity of pain, wipe the weapon clear of prints, place the weapon in the victim's hand to suggest the trite and predictable suicide of a motel recluse, smear crude words on the walls in the victim's blood as evidence of his final cult-related frenzy, take his supply of Dylar, slip back to the car, take the expressway to Blacksmith's, leave Stover's car in Treadwell's garage, shut the garage door, walk home in the rain and the fog. (311)

Jack memorizes and glories in the "plan" and the description for the same reason we do: we all have the details committed to memory from television, from theaters, countless murder scenes overwhelming any specific actions or thoughts. The action is no longer important. In fact, Mink is no longer important. He has lost his potency to a system of information and language so utterly dispersed that his usually, symbolic role, that of antagonist, no longer exists. Late capitalism settles Mink in the discourses of media-babble and consumer culture: "This is the point, as opposed to emerging coastlines, continental plates. Or you can eat natural grains, vegetables, eggs, no fish, no fruit" (311), meaningless chatter characteristic of the Baudrillardian "delirium" of communication and the giddy pleasure at the sign's losing its referent. What is important is an understanding of oneself with a system of images and screens. When Jack says "hail of bullets" Mink hits the floor, when Jack says "Fusillade," Mink ducks and covers, as if a bomb is approaching. Words have replaced actions, representation has replaced the real.

All past plot trajectories dissolve, and that is in itself why writing, or representation, is at the heart of the postmodern predicament. Jack's take on plots is this: "All plots tend to move deathward. This is the nature of plots. Political plots, terrorist plots, lovers' plots, narrative plots" (26). But the summation is followed up by questions adrift: "Is this true? Why did I say it? What does it mean" (26)? Death no longer provides any meaningful telos for plots.

One of the legacies of the period following WWII is that nuclear anxiety has pervaded an epoch. However, this "infection" is not what one might think. Rather than an apocalyptic vision, it has turned into a kind of death and violence that infects every sphere of human life until it is part of the hum of ordinary, daily activity:

> "What if death is nothing but sound?"
> "Electrical noise."
> "You hear it forever. Sound all around. How awful."
> "Uniform, white." (198).

As Heinrich says to Steffie, the enormity of contemporary nuclear capabilities is almost beyond imagining:

> The thing you have to understand about giant stars is that they have actual nuclear explosions deep inside the core. Totally forget these Russian IBMs that are supposed to be so awesome. We're talking about a hundred million times bigger explosions. (233)

To which the only response is: "There was a long pause. No one spoke. We went back to eating for as long as it took to bite off and chew a single mouthful of food" (233). No impact. Material for consumption.

DeLillo stages three displacements of nuclear apocalypse. *White Noise* shows us, as I have argued, how he juxtaposes modernist against postmodernist narrative strategies in the same way that he juxtaposes uses of technology and consumer-culture versions of psychic crises. These stories are and are not about war. They show us the ways in which all master narratives dissolve in the face of a violence that has been packaged for public consumption and entertainment. The oedipal trajectory hasn't a chance; in a thermonuclear blast, or in the breakdown of mass into particles and waves, the story scatters and its characters dissolve into floating and displaced narratives. This is not a good thing or a bad thing, more like a threshold for narrative, identity and culture, a stream of possibilities.

By reading displacements of nuclear war distanced from killing and death through signification we begin to learn new configurations for both narrative and the story of war. The new questions that surface in such a novel are about spatial relationships and representation: *where* does that leave writing, *where* does that leave reading, *where* does that leave human subjectivity? DeLillo seems to say, in a contingent liminality, a postmodern condition which interpretation fails to resolve. That failure is the precise position where new questions might yet be allowed to surface, if we can learn to bear the fact that "we" are moving waves, images, noise, unresolved stories chasing particles and selves for meaning.

NOTES

1. Examples are also available in film, television and opera, for instance, *Testament, The Day After,* and *Einstein on the Beach*, respectively. Peter Schwenger argues in "Writing the Unthinkable" that the arms race and the nuclear legacy that followed it have generated the dominant condition of our time.

CHAPTER V
War, Sexuality, and Narrative

W̲HEN KATHY ACKER WROTE THAT WAR IS A MIRROR OF OUR SEXUALITY IN HER NOVEL *Empire of the Senseless* (1988), she meant for us to call to mind a dual vision of history. On the one hand, the story of war and the story of sexuality are different from one another in that one is destructive of human life and the other productive. But Acker scrutinizes power relationships inside stories of war in order to reveal how war and sexuality are also stories that are continually reinforcing one another. Acker zooms in on processes of war as colonization and decolonization. In particular, Acker borrows the model of colonization and decolonization that emerges in the work of Franz Fanon. As a thematic apparatus, Acker begins where Fanon left off, with an understanding of contemporary society as the result of a whole series of wars—wars of race, class and economy. In his book *A Dying Colonialism* (1965), Fanon outlines the inner history of struggle between France and Algeria with a broader struggle that stretches around the whole of humanity:

> Today the great systems have died or are living in a state of crisis. And it is no longer the age of little vanguards. The whole of humanity has erupted violently, tumultuously onto the stage of history, taking its own destiny in its hands. Capitalism is under siege, surrounded by a global tide of revolution. And this revolution, still without a center, without a precise form, has its own laws, its own life, and depth of unity—accorded it by the same masses who create it, who live it, who inspire each other from across boundaries, give each other spirit and encouragement, and learn from their collective experiences. (1)

Acker's formal use of Fanon's texts raises a set of interesting questions about violence and the novel, and it is that set of questions that are the material of this chapter. Part of my discussion focuses on Acker's insistance on the metaphor of colonization, a formal feature that has yet to be fully accounted for by critics of her work.

Empire of the Senseless stages two parallel versions of colonization: the shifting territory of power and economy as it acts on the individual in society and the shifting territory of identity as it acts on the individual in search of a psycho-sexual foothold. In other words, Acker writes two stories on top of one another, the story of empire building and the story of identity building, in order to show us something about each. For Acker, economic empire building in all its patriarchal forms is a continual war against civilian society because it relies on the colonization of disenfranchised individuals. In her fiction, the story riding alongside that one proposes that identity building is reinforced by the same patriarchal forms that sustain empire building, as I will show. In this chapter I will trace Acker's terms of war: colonization and sexual identity. Taking us through the very terms of the debate on postmodernism, Acker figures the changing modes of power and economy figured by capitalism and the changing modes of pscyho-sexual development as perpetual war stories carried out in particularly discursive terms. *Empire of the Senseless* challenges representation itself to account for the disjunctions and contradictions of a postmodern moment, both for the individual and for culture. As Acker puts it in her novel *Don Quixote*, loving and fucking are always alive in the political realm: "By loving another person, she would right every manner of political, social, and individual wrong" (9).

As many critics have pointed out, in Acker's earlier works such as *The Childlike Life of the Black Tarantula by the Black Tarantula* (1975), *The Adult Life of Toulouse Lautrec by Henri Toulouse Lautrec* (1975), and *Don Quixote*(1986), she insisted on locating "The Father" as a personal nexus of power, repression, and symbolic meaning. Robert Siegle argues in "A Sailor's Life in the Empire of the Senseless" that *Empire* represents the logical extension of the earlier novels. According to Siegle, it translates the power inherent in the "Law of the Father," to the patriarchal forms figured by her narrative versions of capitalism. There is nearly always a daughter in tension with Acker's fathers, and in most cases, the daughter's goal is to overcome or survive the power that the father represents. In nearly all of Acker's works the relationship between father and daughter forms a kind of threshold where identity will either form or be destroyed. In his essay "Kathy Acker's *Don Quixote*: Nomad Writing" Douglas Shields Dix argues that realization concerning the flux of identity is a first step in the quest to escape patriarchy, while later steps include the recognition of economy as the only form of social organization. Naomi Jacobs identifies some key progressions in Acker's fiction in "Kathy Acker and the Plagiarized Self" by tracing how history and identity become more and more textual issues which must be plagiarized, stolen, pirated away from patriarchal culture, suggesting that writing is a revolutionary strategy for escaping economic inscription. *Don Quixote* takes us to the edge of identity collapse in a way by showing us a series of escape processes that rely on questions about war, colonization, and identity:

War, Sexuality, and Narrative

"Where shall I go?" Don Quixote, wandering, woofed questioningly to nobody. "Is anywhere in this world of despair, this post-war endo-colonizations, some where?" (103)

Where *Don Quixote* leaves off, *Empire* launches into a set of questions about identity tied to sexuality and war by figuring them through the terms colonization and decolonization. Though few critics of Acker's work have identified the historical or narrative origin for her interest in colonization, the basis of *Empire* is most recognizable in Acker's earlier work, *Algeria* (1984). In it she uses the Algerian revolution as a kind of narrative ground zero where the story of war and the story of the psycho-sexual development of a girl collide. As I will discuss more specifically later in this discussion, Acker's use of two texts about the atrocities during the French colonization of Algeria and the Algerian revolution serve as the foundation for her novel *Empire of the Senseless* (and were already at work in her earlier publication). The first and perhaps most important question to ask, then, is why Acker insisted on the Algerian historical situation as a model. As I work through this question in my discussion, I will be testing the thesis that Acker found her best and strongest metaphor for sexual colonization at the level of the family in models of national colonization. What is perhaps most interesting is that Acker chose to illuminate her ideas by subordinating thematic concerns to formal ones.

A second element that critics of Acker have yet to account for is the formal significance of her appropriations. The two most important results of her appropriations include the embedding of the story of the desiring father and the sexualized daughter within the story of colonization and decolonization in Algeria, including the texts of Franz Fanon and Pierre Guyotat, and the importance of a French literary tradition that emphasized the link between sexuality and violence and the importance of transgression as a form of resistance, including the work of de Sade, Genet, Artaud, Bataille, Fanon, and Guyotat, texts which deeply inform *Empire of the Senseless* as well as other works.

In order to approach these issues I will be tracing the formal strategy of narrative appropriation. In particular, I am using the term narrative appropriation to mean an anti-mimetic and deconstructive form of doubling and/or borrowing previously existing textual and historical material. Most critics on Acker agree that her dominant formal mode is the appropriation of famous literary texts as well as master narratives of science, philosophy, religion and art that characterized humanism (Jacobs 50; Siegle 71-75; Friedman 37-40). I would like to look first at the way Acker decreates the historical situation of the Algerian revolution with a recreation of that revolution in postapocalyptic France. Appropriating the texts of Franz Fanon and Pierre Guyotat, Acker takes the theme of colonization and translates it into war at the level of colonization and decolonization as formal questions. By showing the way the terms of empire-building, or colonizer and colonized, are, among other things, written ones, Acker begins to trace the ways in which a culture's identity and an individual's identity are always a matter of colonization, reading, and writing.

A more subtle formal feature that I will be discussing in Acker's work is narrative pastiche. In order to teach us how to read colonization of the underclass and colonization of the self as parallel stories, Acker not only appropriates the work of writers such as Frantz Fanon, she also incorporates his "textual" practices into her own narrative through a particularly postmodern version of pastiche. As many contemporary critiques have pointed out, the postmodern use of pastiche has its roots in the convention of parody, but differs in aim. For instance, in "Postmodernism and Consumer Society" in *Modern Drama* Fredric Jameson writes that pastiche is one of the most important formal features of postmodernism and defines it as the imitation of a unique style with completely neutral aims, in contrast to parody:

> Pastiche is, like parody, the imitation of a peculiar or unique style, the wearing of a stylistic mask, speech in a dead language: but it is a neutral practice of such mimicry, without parody's ulterior motive, without the satirical impulse, without laughter, without that still latent feeling that there exists something *normal* compared to which what is being imitated is rather comic. Pastiche is blank parody. (1130)

According to Jameson, what we think of as modernist texts were predicated on the emergence of a grand style, utterly unique to its maker, emphasizing a certain version of originality in art. For instance, a page from Faulkner would be identifiable as such, or one from Joyce or Woolf. A Picasso image or a Frank Lloyd Wright building would be immediately recognizable as such and connected to a certain notion of originality and a unique self. Parody of such a style would, in the same terms, be recognizable. Pastiche, on the other hand, may be located as a historically specific postmodern strategy because it is reinforced by the post-structuralist notion that, as Jameson puts it, personal identity and original style are dead, a thing of the past:

> In a world where stylistic innovation is no longer possible, all that is left is to imitate dead styles, to speak through the masks and with the voices of the styles in the imaginary museum. (1134)

Naomi Jacobs argues in "Kathy Acker and the Plagiarized Self" that the postmodern novel differs from the modernist novel less in terms of narrative technique than in its allegiance to and excavation of critical theory. Jacobs claims that "American postmodernists have drawn upon post-structuralist theories of language and identity both as the basis for technical experiments and as a frequent topic in their works" (50). Nearly all critics who address Acker's work find a fundamental link between her novels and post-structuralist theories (Siegle 73-5; Friedman 37-40; Dix 57). I would disagree with

Jacobs by pointing out that the central formal techniques that Acker uses, pastiche and appropriation, differs radically from modernist precedents. Furthermore, I would like to extend Jameson's definition of postmodern pastiche by looking at Acker's specific use of mimicry and imitation, a unique strategy sometimes referred to in Acker criticism as plagiarism and other times as "pirating" or "theft." I would argue that Acker takes the idea of blank parody, or postmodern pastiche that I talked about earlier, and renders it as a form of plagiarism that not only destablizes concepts of authorship, ownership, and originality, but also transgresses the literary "law," if you will, by breaking a code of professional authorship (no citations, no footnotes, no acknowledgment of sources or borrowed material).

Before I begin my formal study it helps to ask whether the modern/postmodern distinction is a useful one in terms of framing my discussion. Sexuality and war are not postmodern inventions. Clearly literature has showed us how the personal and the political are always in some relationship to one another, from Greek drama to Dante to Shakespeare to Oliver Stone. Furthermore, many past novelists of war addressed the link between sexuality and violence, including but not limited to Conrad, Hemingway, Joyce, Woolf , H.D. and Stein. I mention modernist novelists in particular because it is with the modernist novel of war that a certain notion of the construction of sexuality, namely Freudian, first emerged as part of a larger story of war. Hemingway frequently spoke of the close proximity of violence and intimacy, and Virginia Woolf wrote consistently about the position of woman inside the story of male warfare. This is an important feature to examine in my study because Acker takes on the Freudian family romance, and in particular the Oedipal plot-line, as a patriarchal form of colonization. In the previous chapters I have tried to argue that we add war as a theme and as a formal question to the modern/postmodern discussion, because I believe its shifting forms and content helps us to historicize the literary postmodern, among other things. I have also suggested that by looking at the contemporary novel of war we can begin to see how it is that contemporary culture is the inevitable construct of a whole series of wars. I would now like to take on the formal features of pastiche and appropriation as specific narrative strategies that can *only* be postmodern.

In literary criticism, postmodernism is nearly always set against or in relation to modernism (Huyssen 4-7; Jameson 1-3; McHale 23). But as Lawrence Cahoone charts in *From Modernism to Postmodernism*, the term modernism refers to all kinds of variable ideas from the period between 1914 and 1960. There remains, however, a fair amount of agreement concerning the literary postmodern in terms of formal differences from modernism. For instance, where modernist narrative emphasized the release of objectivity as a narrative aim as well as the transcendent possibilities of art as it works to idealize its subject, the postmodern novel, by contrast, emphasizes formal strategies that foreground how the socio-political organization of modernity has changed in fundamental ways. I have discussed in earlier chapters how writers such as Joyce, Hemingway, and Woolf stand as exemplary models in relation to modernist formal features, particularly in their narrative strategies exhibited in their war narratives. Whether or not modernity has ended or is merely undergoing serious changes, my argument is that one can chart formal differences in the postmodern novel that reflect deep modulations in the organization of culture at the end of the twentieth century as well as the opening of the twenty-first, modulations reflected in the organization of war and the novel. Nearly all of Acker's novels ask how the *forms* we live and die by are changing.

There are several different narrative frames for reading *Empire*, but the most important one appears to be war. In *Suburban Ambush: Downtown Writing and the Fiction of Insurgency,* Siegle identifies the frame for the novel as being characterized by a numbed attitude concerning the imagined, future apocalypse of Western culture: "Those expecting bombs bursting in a thermonuclear glare are likely to be disappointed, for Armageddon is spiritual, not military, and is marked by the retreat from dreams to surfaces" (107). While I agree with Siegle's general comments concerning the structure of this story, I would like to make a somewhat different argument. It is not necessarily the case that "bombs bursting in a thermonuclear glare," images characteristic of postmodern novels such as Pynchon's *Gravity's Rainbow* or even DeLillo's *White Noise* have disappeared. Rather, bombs and battles are taken from the geographic realm to the textual, the psychological and the bodily realm, displaced onto a different territory, a war zone in which sexuality and subjectivity are the front lines. While sexuality and subjectivity may always be part of the production of war, they are not always self-consciously represented as such in the novel. In other words, Acker's novel gives us war as a question of identity by asking what is sexuality or what is a subject: "War, if not the begetter of all things, certainly the hope of all begetting and pleasures. For the rich and especially for the poor. War, you mirror of our sexuality" (26).

One can list many modernist writers who struggled with the issues of war and its effect on identity—cultural and individual. As feminist scholarship in the last ten to fifteen years has evidenced, Virginia Woolf's work is unique because it focused on the centrality of war to aesthetic practice. I am thinking in particular of the work of Jane Marcus, Naomi Black, and the 1991 collection of critical essays *Virginia Woolf and War*, edited by Mark Hussey. I would like to take the time to detour from Acker long enough to describe Woolf's work because a very important distinction about war and sexuality figured by modernism and postmodernism is at stake.

Woolf insisted again and again on linking war and sexuality by dramatizing their relationship through the patriarchal oppression of women, particularly inside the story of marriage. One might categorize her thematic narrative strategies by saying that she often *juxtaposed* sexuality with war and other forms of violence. For example, in *Three Guineas* Woolf focused on the oppression women have encountered in the private and public world along-

War, Sexuality, and Narrative 81

side the tyranny of war. Woolf went as far as to claim that the nineteenth-century woman and the twentieth-century male are "fighting the same enemy" (102). In *To The Lighthouse* Minow-Pinkey says, "what is literally destroying the house is rain, rats and wind, but what is figuratively destroying it is the First World War" (99), implying that the inner, feminine, domestic space is being invaded by war. War is dramatized as an event that occurs not only at the front but also as an invasion into gendered categories such as the home:

> But slumber and sleep though it might there came later in the summer ominous sounds like the measured blows of hammers dulled on felt, which, with their repeat shocks still further loosened the shawl and cracked the teacups. (201)

In other words, symbols of feminine identity, the home, slumber, the shawl and tea-cups, are juxtaposed to the sounds of war: "ominous sounds like the measured blows of hammers."

Another way in which Woolf addresses the thematic relationship between sexuality and war by using strategies of juxtaposition happens in encounters between men and women. As Helen Wussow argues in "War and Conflict in *The Voyage Out*," "sexual encounters between men and women in a patriarchal society frequently take on the dynamics of physical violence and international conflict" (105). As an example, Wussow cites a scene from *The Voyage Out* in which Dalloway's attempts at communication transmit as a form of sexual assault:

> "Girls are kept very ignorant, aren't they? Perhaps it's wise—perhaps— You *don't* know?"
> He spoke as if he had lost consciousness of what he was saying.
> "No; I don't," she said, scarcely speaking above her breath. (68-9)

Wussow goes on to chart how these scenes that dramatize the power play between men's speech and action and women's silence and repression connect with the war raging around them and the silence of the home.

A different version of this notion, in which the treatment of women is connected to the structure of war in *The Voyage Out*, is dramatized when Helen Ambrose disturbs her social group by exclaiming that "it seemed wrong to her, as wrong to keep sailors as to keep a Zoo, and that as for dying on a battlefield, surely it was time we ceased to praise courage" (69). Her statement comes from her observation of warships passing by: "the warships drew past, casting a curious effect of discipline and sadness upon the waters (69). Her views are met with shock and fear, shock from her disagreeing with the men and fear that she will be somehow jettisoned from her proper social place. Deadening restrictions placed on women by patriarchy and marriage are juxtaposed with commentary on militarism.

In addition to many, many thematic examples of Woolf's strategies of juxtaposing sexuality to war, not the least of which are her two books dedicated to the theme of World War, *Three Guineas* and *Between the Acts*, Woolf also experimented with formal strategies that conflated the violence of war with novelistic structure, such as the inclusion of journalism and telegraphy as formal features in *To The Lighthouse*. So while Woolf's clear thematic emphasis on the relationship between sexuality and war is evident in much of her work, I would argue that her formal devices also marked the beginning of a set of narrative strategies that would find their most magnified forms *after* World War II, a historical period in which, as Andreas Huyssen argues in *After the Great Divide*, a depoliticization of culture and art and a canonization of the historical avant garde and modernism after World War II jettisoned everything that came after 1945 into a realm of "futile battle" (4) between critics, severing aesthetic from political forms, or at least seeming to.

The narrative site where Kathy Acker's novel intersects Woolf's is at the story of war and sexuality. What makes *Empire* different from those earlier modernist representations of war is a question of form. The novel is built out of a series of appropriated philosophical, literary, historical and narrative fragments that are juxtaposed and shift at a very rapid pace. For example, one may find the texts of Franz Fanon (103), Sigmund Freud (45), William Burroughs (164), the Marquis de Sade (116), Pierre Guyotat (3-4), and the novel Huckleberry Finn (209) appropriated throughout the novel. Less explicity appropriated are the "texts" of Romanticism and German philosophy (12), ancient Greek philosophy and literature (68), and French feminism (127). These appropriated texts are cut up and pieced together, both referencing and dislocating material from stable historic markers.

Empire of the Senseless is divided into three sections that document the colonization of the individual. Part one, which has five sections, is the subject of this chapter. "Elegy for the World of the Fathers" stages a move from the private and family to the social and symbolic realm. The oppressive Law of the Father experienced by the subject is transformed in this section as the patriarchy of economic systems of power. As Siegle writes in *Suburban Ambush*, "that personal metaphor of the cultural father is displaced by a 'they' as corporate and invisible as a board of directors" (107). Part two, "Alone," performs the subject's struggle with the possible forms available for identity constitution. Part three, "Pirate Night" is divided between two methods of transport for identity in a world in which identity has been all but obliterated.

I used the phrases "performs the subject's struggle" and "transport for identity" above in order to make the claim that the characters in this novel are transitional and provisional. In other words, they change, mutate, trade identities and duplicate themselves across the plain of the text. There are two main and one supporting character in the novel. Abhor is the mutating female in the story. Thivai is Abhor's arch rival, the male always seeking to rob her of an "I," the male in competition for rights to agency and subjec-

War, Sexuality, and Narrative

tivity. A third character, Agone, surfaces briefly in the novel.

Unlike Woolf's emphasis on showing us the close proximity of violence to aesthetic practices, Acker represents them as inextricable. Unlike Woolf's claim that war "came into the house" or the private sphere, Acker represents war as an invasion into sexuality. Unlike Woolf's critiques of militarism, Acker defines war through colonization and sexuality. Given that I am charting formal instances of colonization in this study, I would like to look first at an example of Fanon as a primary text from which Acker appropriates material. In Fanon's three most influential books on the topic of decolonization, *The Wretched of the Earth*, *Black Skin, White Masks*, and *A Dying Colonialism*, it is the 1965 text (*A Dying Colonialism*) that most strikingly appears in *Empire of the Senseless*. In the book Fanon sets up an argument about decolonization that has as its premise the breakdown of the figures of the father and the family. According to Fanon, General de Gaulle's statement in a speech addressed to extremists in which he declared that "Papa's Algeria is dead" (32) is to be taken literally, and he uses the notion of a dead father as a starting point for his discussion. Appropriating de Gaulle's statement, he argues that the role of the father as head of a family household radically changed during the Algerian revolution. He writes: "The old stultifying attachment to the father melts in the sun of the Revolution" (101), and he goes on to address the role of the Algerian woman, particularly the role of the daughter, in order to make claims about the structure of colonization and changes in the family that happened as a result of the Algerian revolution. It is as if Fanon must begin with the structure of the family in order to articulate the structure of war, specifically the oppression of the ruling government and the revolutionary history of the oppressed peoples. As new roles emerge, the son and the daughter are replaced by the "militant" and the "woman-as-arsenal," and the old paternal order collapses:

> The old paternal assurance, already shaken, would collapse once and for all. The father no longer knew how to keep his balance . . . It was during this period that the father buried the old values and decided to follow along the new path. (103)

The "new path" that Fanon speaks of is a new family in which the authority of the father is seen as a residual effect of the colonizers. Destabilized from his position of authority, the family is restructured around the revolutionary force of the children as soldiers, a move echoed by Lessing, Acker, and Silko. Fanon even goes as far as to describe the fall of the father as a combat situation: "This defeat of the father by the new forces that were emerging [the children] could not fail to modify the relations that had formerly prevailed in Algerian society" (105).

In the section of part one "Let the Algerians Take Over Paris," Acker employs her strongest pastiche-appropriations of Fanon's *A Dying Colonialism*. Specifically, Acker lifts the plot of his story of colonization and decolonization in terms of the family. The evidence is first chartable at the level of the sentence. For example, on a page describing the Algerian's impoverishment at the hands of Europeans, Acker inserts "Papa Death wailed on a street corner" (71), appropriating Fanon's use of de Gaull. Acker goes on to use the name and the figure of "Papa Death" as a patriarchal figure. Similarly, Fanon writes that the spirit of revolution rests in the mouths and stories of the women revolutionaries who will be "grandmothers of the future"; Acker writes: "I could hear the old women. My grandmothers" (68), who she later desribes as "the future." Acker repeatedly inserts pieces from Fanon's analyses of colonization and decolonization, appropriated from his text *The Wretched of the Earth*. For instance, Fanon writes that in 1956 "Lacoste instituted urban and rural militias . . . as a necessity for order and as a means of security" (90). Acker recasts this language and text and places it in the middle of a story about a daughter's encounter with a surrogate father figure, "the old man." Almost from nowhere the text appears and disappears:

> The French in the past and under the new right-wing regime said that "doing what was necessity" in order to control the Algerians was "on the part of their country . . . not a war for riches or local aggrandizement but a war for security." (68)

Earlier I noted Fanon's use of General de Gaull's phrase, "Papa Algeria," as well as Acker's appropriation. Perhaps the most important pastiche-appropriation related to Franz Fanon is centered on the character of Abhor and her encounter with a "corpse old white guy" in the section "Let the Algerians Take Over Paris." Acker appropriates Fanon's description of what happens to a daughter inside the family structure in the face of revolution. Again from *A Dying Colonialism*, Fanon writes that daughters, who were previously—as in pre-revolution—defined by their value as potential mothers and wives, and thus raised to be married into another family as soon as they hit puberty, underwent a change based on a value system connected to their new, potentially revolutionary roles. According to Fanon, "The woman-for-marriage progressively disappeared, and gave way to the woman-for-action" (108), the militant. Furthermore, the daughter's new role outside the older paternal authority of the family includes the notion that "The men's words were no longer the law" (109). Fanon argues that changes in the family and in sexuality paralleled the structure of the war between colonizer and colonized:

> Algerian society in the fight for liberation, in the sacrifices that it was willing to make in order to liberate itself from colonialism, renewed itself and developed new values governing sexual relations. The woman ceased to be a complement for man inside the family. *She literally forged a new place for herself by her sheer strength.* (109)

The text of a newly emerged daughter figure, described by Fanon as a woman who "would sleep in the forests or in the grottoes, who would roam the djebel dressed as a man, with a gun in her hands" (109) broke from the authority of the father since all former taboos and prohibitions were dissolving: "His [the father's] old fear of dishonor had become altogether absurd in the light of the immense tragedy being experienced by his people" (108). Remarkably, not only does Fanon theorize a new position for the father, son, and daughter in the family, he goes on to suggest that the daughter turns back to the father and invites him to "undergo a kind of mutation, to wrench himself free of himself" (110) and to let go of his "Old values, sterile and infantile phobias" (110).

Acker's pastiche-appropriation of Fanon in *Empire* takes the form of Abhor's encounter with a dying father: "He was old, the Parisian, and white . . . 'Come visit, child,' the man said" (66). As Abhor is talking with this old man, she remembers a flashback of herself at puberty. From page 66 to page 73 the reader encounters pastiche-appropriations from Fanon mixed with psychoanalytic terminology characteristic of the oedipal scenario as the daughter faces off with the father. The two stories, both empty of historical meaning, blend to make a third story, one in which the dying father and the dying colonialism are rendered in particularly sexual terms: "When I was just at the age of fucking, so to speak, puberty . . . he told me while he was sobbing that every man wanted to use me. Except for himself. Crying steadily he reached for my tits" (67).

As Acker moves from occupied Paris to memories of puberty, she uses appropriated textual material as modes of transtition. For instance, there is a gun between the old man and Abhor during their conversation, an object which Acker uses to connect appropriations: "I looked around me. I didn't see anyone but a gun. Maybe most people are trying to imitate their controllers" (72). The same gun is represented in a sexually charged passage as resting between father and daughter on a bed: "He balanced the gun on one knee while his other hand fondled a long needle" (69). During the conversation, Abhor wrestles with the idea that this father-figure is both begetter and that which she must reject. The form that this struggle takes centers around the gun. The old man tries to persuade Abhor to double suicide with him on a bed, a sexually loaded proposition: "One must learn how to suicide in this world, for that's all that's left us" (69). In Fanon's text, the daughter remade with a gun in her hands "would look at the father, she would sit facing the father, would speak to him" (109) in a way that both would reflect their new roles. The daughter would "invite the father to undergo a kind of mutation, to wrench himself free of himself" (110). Fanon's militant daughter emerges in Acker's text, the daughter who would sleep in the forests or in the grottoes, who would roam the djebel dressed as a man, with a gun in her hands. Much in the manner that Fanon described fathers and daughters, Abhor understands the position of the father as one whose authority is dying:

"If history does make us," I spat at the goat and said, "if those who are older than us formed us, you're a walking disease . . . He didn't look at me. I think he saw me for the first time as more than an object of killing in the same manner as a lover suddenly notices that the obsession's a person. Humaness shocks. (69)

Another example of pastiche-appropriation concerns doubling the text of a woman's role in culture. According to Fanon, mothers and grandmothers underwent a change as the patrilineal society was challenged through violence and war: "Algerian mother . . . grandmother, the aunt and the "old woman" (37) were reborn, and their positions marked a movement in which the Algerian male and the colonial administration battled to define the role of women. Fanon argues that the figure of woman became a battle front between colonizer and colonized: "In the colonialist program, it was the woman who was given the historical mission of shaking up the Algerian man" (38), and in the Algerian revolution, it was the same woman who was given the historical mission of attacking the colonialist fathers. Acker references the figure of the "old woman" as an emblem of war several times in her novel:

Though the whites had cut out their tongues, though they had neither been allowed to speak for themselves even as children, though only drool and vomit had ever dropped out of their mouths: from out of the mouths of these old women whose cunts were now caves, the banners of war emerged. (68)

Put slightly differently, this pastiche-appropriated textual material does not function in a narrative sense to further the plot or develop a character. Instead it functions to reference and then dislocate historical material so that its thematic impact is subordinated to its formal function in the novel. That formal function, pastiche-appropriation, serves to show us how Fanon's vision of decolonization and Acker's vision of war and sexuality are parallel stories. In the case of Fanon, the text is tied to a certain notion of historical specificity—the Algerians were tortured at the hands of the French colonizers. In the case of Acker, by doubling and flattening the historical material, the borders of history and representation are dissolving and an ordinarily repressed story about a daughter's psycho-sexual development emerges. Let me emphasize that my reading in no way suggests that Acker is devaluing or trivializing the historically specific events recorded by Fanon. On the contrary, she shows us how the violence theorized by Fanon may be traced in the discourses of postmodern fiction, because the formal features of her novel highlight the discursive war of one group of people—"fathers"—against daughters. Using pastiche-appropriation, Acker seems to be making the argument that it is only through a variety of texts that we may detect the complex operations of colonization. In other words, Fanon's text, along with all other discourses on colonization such as the colonization of meaning in the novel, or the colonization of daughters, and including fictional language—each must be activated in order for a reader to detect anything useful about colonization. It is as if Acker is claiming that it is only through the story of colonization that we can view the war within sexuality. As Fanon writes, the Algerian woman emerges unveiled as a "link, sometimes an essential one, in the revolutionary machine" (60), and, machine-like, carrying weapons against her body, she enters the city, the prison, torture and death as the carrier of bombs, genades, and weaponry "bound to her body by a whole system of strings and straps" (62). Abhor, part machine, part sexual terrorist, emerges from the city, gun in hand, in conflict with her own body in particularly Fanonian terms: "Joining the horde of Dervish camp followers and ex-whores trailing along in the wake of the North African . . . infantry women and soldiers of the Legion, throwing away my useless high-heel shoes" (83), the women "set splinters" under the owners' fingernails and set fire to them.

At the end of the Algerian Revolution in *Empire of the Senseless*, the Algerians win Paris "so they would own something" (83). Abhor remarks, "We looked at Paris which was now a third world" (82). Appropriating Fanon's use of the term "bosses" to indicate the French colonizer figures in Algeria, Acker has her characters ask, "What are we going to do now that we don't have a boss"(82)? In "A Few Notes on Two of My Books," Acker writes that when the Algerians take over Paris there is a society not defined by the oedipal script, which she defines as a Freudian, phallocentric one in which total domination on the political, economic, social and personal levels reigns. Unlike a character from Woolf, Acker's characters experience conflict inside their own bodies. For instance, the figure of the mutating daughter as she moves from violence to violence stands in formally for Fanon's argument in *A Dying Colonialism* that colonialism settles itself in the individual and works to expel a self, to the extent that an ordinary breath taken by the colonized is "a combat breathing" (65). According to Fanon, the Algerian revolution located the Algerian woman as "inaccessible, ambivalent, with a masochistic component" (64). One could argue that Abhor is precisely such a woman.

It is at this point that I would like to turn from Fanon to Acker's appropriation of Pierre Guyotat's text *Eden, Eden, Eden* (1970). Like *Empire*, the novel's violence is set in an apocalyptic zone of the Algerian desert during civil war, and the text seems to design every act of brutal sex and violence humanly possible. As Roland Barthes writes in the introduction to the novel, Guyotat insisted that the breakdown of language, the breakdown of society as an effect of the war in Algeria, and the structure of sexuality are interdependent movements. Published in France in 1970, the book was banned and censored for just under eleven years under the rationale that it was a pornographic text. What the book actually contains is a nearly unbearable conflation of violence, sexuality and language, and its theme, the atrocities that emerged before and during the Algerian revolution, takes on a new form, an idea I will discuss next. Acker has said that her turn to Guyotat's text was influenced by her understanding of a nexus between power, sexuality and politics. If we go back now and try to understand why the story of Abhor's sexual development opens the book, and why it runs alongside the story of the Algerian revolution, we may yet determine how sexuality and colonization are linked to writing and the body specifically.

Abhor is neither a "true" woman in the biological sense, nor a cybernetic robot, but rather a subject continually generated and erased according to the lines of her culture. She is a daughter undergoing shifts from sexual object, to desiring subject, to revolutionary soldier, to nomad. One story, the story of civilization, the family, patriarchy, and the order of the ruling, economic class is actually at war with another story, the personal story of whether or not the individual daughter will survive: "Rather than being autistic dumb feelingless ice, I would like the whole apparatus—family and memory—to go to hell"(52). As Abhor moves through the violences in her culture, sexual and economic, the choice that she faces is between living in a master-slave relationship, characterized by rape, or living in a sort of soldier-whore position in which life is predicated on various forms of transgression: "I want to kill the person I love so that I can be dead. This seemed to be an apt response to the world"(53); "Most of the prisoners, after they've been beaten and tormented, prefer giving head to being dead" (86).

In Guyotat's *Eden, Eden, Eden* we find a similar girl under revision. For example, early on in the novel a soldier violently rapes a young girl while her father is pinned to the floor, tortured, and forced to watch. In what might be the most graphic conflations of sexuality and violence in all of literature, Guyotat erases the possibility of distancing oneself from the act of sex and the act of war by giving us a formal prison—the entire novel is written as a single sentence. The scene of the daughter's rape is conflated horribly with the language of war:

> Sweat oozing on bare chest, waking girl: girl gazing, into soldier's mouth panting open . . . soldier standing girl up, squashed against wire fence of kennel, squeezing, kissing mouth, cavities of ears susurrating with bloody cerumen; soldier's hand unbuttoning dungarees, pulling out member; girl eyes closed, hands spread out on fence . . . straw-dust disturbed rising around legs, injecting girl with clear, hot jissom . . . fence collapsing; soldier folding, covering girl's body . . . RIMA squad dragging woman . . . (4)

It is as if language cannot get away from the violence because, as Barthes argues in the introduction to the book, mimesis has given way to a reciprocal metonymy in which language, violence and sexuality are indissoluble. Violent sexual terms such as "mouth panting open," "squeezing, kissing mouth," and "sweat oozing" are terribly conflated with phrases with a military echo such as "squashed against wire fence," "soldier's hand," "fence collapsing," "solider folding," and "RIMA squad." After the rape of the daughter

War, Sexuality, and Narrative

in this early scene, the daughter is transformed into a "girl-whore" who sleeps with the enemy and with the revolutionaries without loyalty to either. Later she is transformed into a terrorist, and in the end to a mother who commits incest with her son. Gone are the strategies of the modernist novel to represent the proximity of war to sexuality. Through the course of a single sentence that never ends a mutating woman emerges.

In Guyotat's novel, feminine figures only emerge as sexual objects subect to violence. The bodies of daughters, whores, terrorists, and mothers are raped, tortured and mutilated throughout the text. As the feminine figure of the daughter, for instance, mutates over the pages of Guyotat's novel, other rapes reconfigure the sexuality and violence in ever-changing terms. As a solider rapes a whore in the Algerian desert, the "terms" of the violence both repeat earlier rapes and deliver different ones: "Jissom spurting from loins . . . coming all over her face . . . a moment of glory . . . a nation . . . slobbering over cheek of whore . . . enormous tongue . . . sweat cooling on fingers" (70). For Guyotat, violent rape is the subtext of war.

Acker may have been the only American woman writer ever to face off with Guyotat on his own terms. Part of what part one of *Empire* attempts is to break the trajectory—psychic, sexual, social, narrative—of the Freudian Oedipal scenario by way of articulating the conflict of mastery as it meets resistance in the feminine. In Freudian terms, the primary task of each human is to master the Oedipus complex in order to achieve psycho-sexual development. In Freud's family romance, then, the woman would need to achieve psycho-sexual individuation through struggling with and repressing the desire she has for her father. One could argue that Acker makes the center of this neurosis the center of her novel, which makes the story of neurosis itself and the nuclear complex of the story, Oedipal. What each new daughter must master, and each of the five sections stages, is an attraction to a "father" that, when juxtaposed with a father's attraction to a daughter, extends into incest.

A combination of the phrases "whore," "war," and "abhorrent," the character of Abhor travels a similar path in Acker's novel. By appropriating the text of a mutating woman from Guyotat, Acker seems to make the argument that the position of the daughter is a nexus where sexuality and violence meet. In other words, in her appropriation of violent rape as a subtext of war from Guyotat, Acker replaces the soldier with the father and colonization with patriarchy in the family. In her first run through the Oedipal script, Acker shows us a daughter as a sexual object. Abhor is raped in quite pornographic terms by her father:

> At the moment my mother was whining, daddy was smelling my cunt. "I've reached my best moment now!" he explained. Now I was sure what he was referring to. "This is the moment of truth!! . . . I'm going off off off jacking it off!!! . . . my hands're gonna be broken from this one!!! . . . I don't even recognize my own body!!! . . . and it doesn't matter!!! . . . I know you're

mine!!! . . . I made you!!! . . . I'm making you!!! . . . I swore I'd live for pleasure!!! . . . My tongue is fucking enormous!!! . . . feel it!!! it's reaching down to my waist!!! . . . You're seeing your actual father in his moment of truth!!! God almighty!!! . . . nothing matters!!! . . . You're my God!!! . . . my daughter: I worship you!!! . . . I beg you to do it, show I can please you!!! . . . now look at it, it's big in my corkscrewing hand!!! . . . kiss it!!! . . . God is in heaven I'm in heaven I've died the whole world in heaven!!! . . . I'm coming all over your face!!! (15)

Borrowing from the horrific conflations in Guyotat, such as "coming all over her face," "a moment of glory," and "enormous tongue," Acker replays the rape of a daugher by a soldier as the rape of a daughter by a father. In addition, Acker dissolves the Oedipal script by transgressing the prohibition against incest. Like the writers with whom she shares the clearest narrative affinity, Acker insists that the story must go where the culture will not. This pornographic scene stands in sharp contrast to Freud's account by showing us what may be repressed in Freud. The Oedipal script participates in the colonization of female bodies by presenting the father as the controlling force in the story of the daughter's sexuality. The daughter in Acker's story, part human, part robot, bursts past the Oedipal scenario, or incest, into life: "I decided to keep on living rather than kill myself" (19). This breaking of the cultural and psychological bloodclot does not accept the symbolic function of the phallus that, say, poststructuralism posits. Abhor either misreads or reads too literally the phallus: "If a man's power resides in his dick" (127) then the dick is the obstacle to overcome. Like the choices outlined in the model of the Algerian revolution, Abhor finds two options: rape and repression, on the one hand, violence and sexual transgression on the other. Sexual transgression in this case is preferable to rape and repression: "I did what I wanted to do. My action now followed my desire. I went to Algeria" (48).

Acker's pastiche-appropriation of Guyotat can be best understood as borrowing an entire stylistic mode. That never ending sentence characteristic of *Eden, Eden, Eden* that traps a reader into a sexually explicit and neverending violence is a narrative mode that Acker employs throughout the novel in smaller pieces. For example, her disrupted grammar sections that conflate voilence, language and sexuality find their strategic roots in texts like Guyotat's, but they differ in that their aim is to represent the psycho-sexual development of an individual inside a culture dominated by economy and violence:

> In my isolation and in my desperation in that dead city chi-chi city city made by and for the bourgeoisie, it seemed to me that my sexuality was a source of pain. That my sexuality was the crossroads not only of my mind and body but of my life and death. My sexuality was ecstasy. It was my desire which, endless, limited neither by a solely material nor by a solely mental reality. In that city dominated by commodities, more and more unsatiated I cried. I would kill the city of perfection. My tears were the tears

of whores. I would have Mary Magdalen tear Virgin Mary's flesh into shreds. My cunt juice and piss, red, would drop out of her eyes. I who am only gentle. I who could not even hurt my mother who hated me. I little baby: my crying my pissing is my sexuality. (65)

Phrases such as "cunt juice and piss," "tears of whores," "sexuality . . . was a source of pain," "sexuality was the crossraods," "sexuality was ecstasy," "I would kill the city," "my crying my pissing is my sexuality," illuminate the psycho-sexual development models that Acker is playing with *within* the texts she has appropriated.

Because Abhor is continually choosing a violent sexual existence over a death by patriarchal domination, "I quickly chose a raped body over a mutilated or dead one" (64), her monologues about sexual identity are full of twists on the Freudian account of sexual development. Like Guyotat, Acker reads colonization as an atrocity only representable through obscene language. It is as if each author is asking us to look at the other side of a nation's act to colonize and a patriarchal culture's act to colonize as the torture and rape of individuals. In other words, each author is claiming that what colonization would look like on paper is a never-ending stream of obscene violence. This is a radically different view on the politics of colonization, and takes both of their texts, as well as many other writers' texts, out of the category of pornographic and puts them into the category of historical fiction, not unlike the genre of the war novel.

In the first section of "Elegy" we are presented with an incest narrative that torqued, or pushed to the extreme, the Oedipal script in "Rape by the Father." A different version of incest happens in the fifth section of "Elegy," interestingly titled "Let the Algerians Take Over Paris." Again conflating the theme of the Algerian revolution with psycho-sexual narratives, Acker reduces and revises the theme of colonizer and colonized. As Abhor describes it, "What I suddenly remembered or knew is that I sexually desired my adopted father" (67). As Abhor admits this desire, the terms of colonizer and colonized dissolve:

At last. I've' been waiting for you for what seems like a really long time. For a second. For a minute. For an hour. For a day. For a month. For a year. I knew you were going to come back to me. To the exact spot where we first met. In a river. In my cunt. I'm sopping wet. Let's fuck on top of this fountain. Splashing the waters of hydrochloric acid into my nostrils. Daddy. (84)

In this version Abhor is not the victim of incest, but rather a desiring female taking pleasure in pain: "I've been waiting for you . . ." "I knew you were going to come back to me." In that sado-masochistic union a border of possibility emerges. Abhor asks the question, "Is a former victim an owner or no thing" (85)? Former owners, the French and the English, the American corporations, as well as fathers, go to "sea" at the end of this section. As the

Algerians take over Paris, the individual version of otherness, Abhor, also bleeds beyond her victim borders in a specifically psycho-sexual re-writing of the Oedipal script. In this version, the former victims—the Algerians *and* a daughter colonized by a father—emerge triumphant not because they win their respective wars through violent combat, but rather because they escape the binary terms that lock individuals and society into war: self and other, father and daughter, executioner and victim, colonizer and colonized. What we ordinarily read as a matter of natural cultural organization is recast as a process by which power oppositions order society.

Clearly one must make room for the problems inherent in Fanon's and Guyotat's texts, and even Acker's, particularly in their definitions of the feminine. While each text may contain moments of liberation and transformation of the feminine, each also brings the reader to a troubling set of terms for women—sexual violence as the only means of escape and identity reconstitution. An excellent book which helps to complicate Fanon's ideas and to situate his ideas within contemporary discussions is *The Fact of Blackness*, edited by Alan Read. In it bell hooks re-reads Fanon's *The Wretched of the Earth* looking in particular for how relations between black males and black females constitutes a site of resistance untheorized by Fanon, but available for scrutiny to contemporary artists, writers and critics. In her essay, "Feminism as a Persistent Critique of History," hooks argues that the damage to colonized peoples carries with it the story of the desiring female, a story that we must work to uncover. Her critique of Fanon points to his desexualisation of the feminine. According to hooks, the female body is rendered undesiring in Fanon:

> Not only is the female body, black or white, always a sexualised body, always not the body that "thinks," but it also appears to be a body that never longs for freedom. Radical subjectivity as Fanon conceives of it is registered in the recognition of that longing to be free. This desire is seen only as present in the hearts of men. (84)

Similarly, from the same anthology, Kobena Mercer argues that a postnationalist subject has psycho-sexual implications that are as yet unaccounted for in Fanon. In her essay "Decolonization and Disappointment," Mercer identifies several psycho-sexual points that both Fanon and contemporary postcolonial theory have tended to overlook, including homosexuality as an anxiety in Fanon's *Black Skin, White Masks*, and the distortions of the feminine inherent in Fanon's claim that sexuality is an anchoring point for the production of relations of oppression between coloniser and colonized (124). The anthology breaks down and reconfigures some of Fanon's main arguments by analyzing the themes available in his story of colonization and decolonization. I am arguing that Acker is doing the same work, but instead approaches that work formally, at the level of narrative pastiche-appropriation.

War, Sexuality, and Narrative

Still, one cannot get around the idea that, like Guyotat, Acker's terms are intimately tied to sexual violence. Does that mean that the bodies and identities of women have nowhere else to go, no choice other than self destruction? Is Acker suggesting that the modernist narrative telos availiable for the woman characters outlined by Gilbert and Gubar, death, madness, or marriage, have only evolved a razor-thin distance with death, madness and sexual violence? I do not believe Acker's texts answer these questions entirely. I do think that Acker goes to great lengths to resist "restoring" some social order in which gender is "repaired" and women are given a better position in society. Rather, it is more likely the case that such a story would cover over the one Acker is trying to reveal. As Robert Siegle argues, Acker's novel shows us what is possible when the dualisms that order the socius break open:

> Interpersonal power is no longer contestable within the model of colonization because its neat binary oppositions between outside and inside, mercantile state and colony, patriarch and daughter, are anachronistic as the too literal melodrama of masters and slaves. (111)

Through her own sexual transgressions, the subject of the remaining sections of the novel, Abhor transgresses categories of desire such as incest, homosexuality, rape, sadomasochism and erotic love, where alternative possibilities to victimhood are available. Her wars are psycho-sexual options, in other words, where the chance to transgress is preferable to the death of accepting cultural inscription. What Acker takes with her that the Oedipal script, Fanon, and Guyotat all left out is female desire in especially unwritten and taboo forms: the desiring daughter, the escaped prisoner, the transgressive revolutionary.

The section "Let the Algerians Take Over Paris," the last of five sections in "Elegy," ends with Abhor making her escape in particularly postmodern terms:

> My father is no longer important cause interpersonal power in this world means corporate power. The multinationals along with their computers have changed and are changing reality. Viewed as organisms, they've attained immortality via-bio-chips. Etc. Who needs slaves anymore? So killing someone, anyone, like Reagan or the top IBM executive board members, whoever they are, can't accomplish anything," I babbled, and I wondered what would accomplish anything, and I wondered if there was only despair and nihilism, and then I remembered . . . In the boat my father I had never known was dead. (83)

As dead fathers drift to sea, Abhor drifts into the desert of post-apocalypse Paris, and the section ends with a kind of freedom to transgress characterized by sex and tattooing, the subjects that open the next section. What Abhor needs to do to continue on her travels involves a specifically postmodern narrative feature: the rejection of nihilism in favor of transitory, ecstatic subjectivity, a built or constructed subjectivity, a mutable, written, and mobile position. The conclusion of the section marks the end of a war written in the terms of colonization and its binary supports and the beginning of Abhor and Thivai's journey into a runaway technology, sexuality, consumer culture and language. Similarly, the end of this section also forecloses the narrative limits of the realist and modernist novels. Abhor need not find the real, nor does she need to secure an autonomous inner self. "Reality is something else, not here," and subjectivity is transitory and mutable.

In the introduction to *Eden, Eden, Eden* Roland Barthes claims that "Criticism, unable to discuss the author, his subject, or his style, can find no way of taking hold of this text" (preface). I find myself in this discussion wanting to make the same claim about Acker's texts. Certainly Acker has challenged the usefulness of literary criticism in more than one interview, suggesting that the texts must be entered and that a reader must participate in the language and make it her own. Since she was also one of the most theoretically informed contemporary fiction writers of the twentieth-century, one must pay close attention to that last call to "make it her own." She did not use critical theory in the way that academia does, to prove or disprove an argument. She used it as material for artistic production. To do that kind of work a critic would need to let the desire to make an argument go in favor of riding/writing the story. Another way to think about it would be to ask what the "use" of an Acker text might be. One way that we can "use" Acker's text is to interrogate the Oedipal script as it informs not just the story of psychosexual development, but also as it informs novelistic narrative and war in terms of a model of patriarchy. The terms of war for Acker no longer have to do with sons and fathers, but rather with daughters and fathers, or the story of all our sexual and psychic development. War, as she so aptly conflates it, mirrors sexuality. Thus, a second "use" involves exposing the dangers of the oedipalization of a subject and a nation. If we can read for the processes by which subjects and nations are written by and through this new understanding of war, perhaps we can also read for ways to write them differently.

Lastly, one might use a novel like Acker's to underscore the specificity of postmodern narrative language and its relationship to war. Acker uses pastiche-appropriation to deform and reform the terms of colonization to reflect a set of textual and sexual intersections. By showing the way the terms of empire building are, among other things, written ones, Acker begins to trace how a culture's identity and an individual's identity are always a matter of writing and war.

However, such "uses" in literary criticism carry with them the very impulses they seek to challenge. We, as deconstructive critics, are not outside the empire of the senseless, we helped make it through the academy, we live in it, we ignore it, we narrate over it. We are included as the recipients of Abhor's hate male/mail:

War, Sexuality, and Narrative

Everytime I talk to one of you, I feel like I'm taking layers of my own epidermis, which are layers of still freshly bloody scar tissue, black brown and red, and tearing each one of them off so more and more of my blood shoots into your face. This is what writing is to me a woman. (210)

In this we become complicit in the critical "wars" surrounding gender studies as well as the postmodern novel. The more we argue about the terms "masculine" and "feminine" or the "truth" or "falsehood" of postmodernism, the less we are able to see the emerging forms that might provide us with new questions about the stories we tell ourselves about identity war. And since the very acts of reading and writing are eveywhere the story of war for Acker, even literary criticism is suspect. Her death writes her life in front of us. Like Fanon's body, her body was in conflict with itself through cultural inscription (symbolically) and disease (biologically). But this was always already a story both of them were trying to tell.

CHAPTER VI
Narrative Fragmentation: Toward an American Resistance Literature

NOT FOR NOTHING HAVE I CHOSEN TO EXIT THIS DISCUSSION WITH KATHY ACKER AND Leslie Marmon Silko. For it is their work that most troubles my position as "literary critic," "woman," and "white." And both of their works resist traditional interpretation as we understand it in the academy. In an interview in 1992 with Linda Niemann for *Women's Review of Books*, Leslie Marmon Silko advised readers how to react to her novel *Almanac of the Dead*: "Read this and be horrified." Unlike two of her more popular novels, *Ceremony* and *Storyteller*, *Almanac of the Dead* is an ugly book. It is ugly because it is angry. In 1992 *The New York Times Book Review* called her prose "ferocious," "defiant," and "scathing." That same year *Time* labeled her vengeful, very angry, raging, and self-righteous. The judgment from *Newsweek* was perhaps most telling when they declared that in her cosmology there are good people and there are white people. These reactions are a good starting point for a discussion of this novel because they emphasize the issue of resistance. I would like to begin by turning the issue of resistance into a formal question. For Silko, the story of Native American resistance is repressed by another story, and that story is the history of the United States.

First and foremost, *Almanac of the Dead* is a novel thematically built around the economic control that the United States has imposed upon its indigenous peoples. Silko represents this control as a perpetual war story. It is written from the point of view of a culture that bears witness to genocide, containment, torture and arrest, or the power of one nation used against another. As such the novel does not easily fit into the trajectory of the war novel as I have been discussing it, and neither does it fit into the category of the literary postmodern, as I will show. For one thing, as a Native American novel, Silko's work is marked by its connection to the "sacred," a term Paula Gunn Allen has used to mean any material that is based on Native cultures' ritual and myth. Furthermore, her work draws its narrative frame from an

97

oral tradition and a Native American ethics that, above all, preserves Pueblo traditions. It is in those definitions of the sacred and preservation that the book begins to resist interpretation, since, as Allen argues, in white culture (and by extension, American institutions such as universities), to preserve means to learn and tell all in the interests of the pursuit of knowledge and objectivity, while in native cultures, preservation means to guard against invasion, to keep secret, to judge the motivations of the person asking the question. According to Allen in her essay "Special Problems in Teaching Leslie Marmon Silko's *Ceremony*," Silko is constantly laying stories alongside her novels that are clan stories, and as such are not to be told outside the clan. So from the start a non-clan reader's attempts to know and chart the stories in Silko's novels might be said to be frustrated by a fundamental formal strategy of resistance embedded in each text. Again, we are drawn to the deeper definitions of resistance in a struggle to build a suitable reading practice for Silko's work. But I do not believe that means non-Native readers ought to put the book away. On the contrary, I believe the non-Native reader ought to trouble their reading and desire to "win an argument" or "form a conclusion."

The narrative frame of *Almanac of the Dead* illuminates the double movement of the book, that is, the laying of stories of clan alongside the history of United States growth. The first difficulty for readers is that the book covers roughly 500 years, and not in chronological order. Ordinary historical markers such as the arrival of Cortez, the Indian wars, Vietnam, and other weighty Western calendar dates are dislocated and relocated in the short, personal narratives of a large number of characters. The second difficulty for readers is characterization. Beginning with elder Native American twin sisters in Tucson who are translating the almanac, the reader must navigate many voices, from drug addicts to corrupt cops and judges, mafia, veterans, arms smugglers, prostitutes and psychics. At first glance such characters appear to have little to do with one another. Eventually, however, distinctions can be made by scutinizing how capitalism inscribes their bodies and their relationship to the land. Alongside characters inscribed by economy we get characters who have a hole in their hearts or stomachs, some who are missing skin or whose skin is diseased. These traits connect to both the land, the only "main" character in the novel, and the almanac, the pages of which are made from horse stomachs. Thus, the story of the indigenous peoples of Mexico and the Americas is set alongside the story of European conquest and capitalist expansion. As sacred myth and ritual merge with capitalist expansion and the economic inscription of identity, a territory of struggle emerges that, like the sacred almanac, has no beginning and no end, no original or stable place in time.

In addition to its connection to the sacred, competing notions of preservation, and distorted form, the novel has specific ethnographic and historical contexts. As such, Silko's novel must be read *against* the war novel for several reasons. Firstly, because its form challenges a Western version of history

Narrative Fragmentation

in which European and American war dates are defining events. Secondly, because its form challenges the genre of the novel in general. Specifically, Silko's text resists a certain version of the form of the novel as it has corresponded to the emergence of capitalist modes of production. As Ian Watt identified, the rise of the novel has been understood as a bourgeois art form that corresponded to developments in the middle class and the formation of social order in nineteenth-century European nation-states. Silko's text shifts from a depiction of class and economy through novelistic language and conventions such as character and setting to the representation of class and economy as character, as I will argue. Lastly, the novel more accurately fits the forms and themes of an American resistance literature, as I will show. For the purposes of this discussion I will be borrowing and expanding a definition charted by Barbara Harlow in her book *Resistance Literature*. In her analysis, Harlow argues that resistance literature is fundamentally distinct from the Western literary canon as we know it since the authors write from a fundamentally different position:

> The distinction presupposes furthermore an "occupying power" which has either exiled or subjugated . . . a given population and has in addition significantly intervened in the literary and cultural development of the people it has dispossesed and whose land it has occupied. Literature, in other words, is presented . . . as an arena of struggle. (2)

Harlow is of course speaking of literary productions linked to the Israeli occupation of the West Bank when she makes this claim. However, as many Native American authors, artists, and scholars have pointed out, the growth of the United States as a nation has a shadow-self; the Native American, Central American, Mexican-American economies, cultures and peoples have each experienced that "growth," to differing degrees, as a from of occupation in precisely Harlow's terms (Garcia 40; Schweninger 49). I would like to extend Harlow's definition by claiming that resistance literature is the other side of, or more precisely, in tension with, the genre of the modern novel of war and the literary postmodern, and must be read against the grain of those genres in terms of form.

As Susan Pérez Castillo has so carefully argued, *Almanac of the Dead* seems to engage the literary postmodern on many levels. For instance, in its flurry of economically inscribed characters, the novel does seem to formally engage the emergence of a new type of social life and economic order, what Fredric Jameson has termed "multinational capitalism." However, Silko traces the start of that order to 1500, while Jameson places the period at about 1960. Another possible postmodern link is in the way the novel is structured in a fragmentary combination of stories that initially propels reading but also blocks it, a formal strategy I have traced in the novels of Larry Heinemann, Don DeLillo, Doris Lessing and Kathy Acker. This idea is perhaps best illuminated by Roland Barthes in "The Death of the Author":

A text is made of multiple writings, drawn from many cultures and entering into mutual relations of dialogue, parody, contestation, but there is one place where this multiplicity is focused and that place is the reader, not, as was hiterto said, the author. The reader is the space on which all the quotations that make up a writing are inscribed without any of them being lost; a text's unity lies not in its origin but in its destination. Yet this destination can no longer be personal: the reader is without history, biography, psychology; he is simply that someone who holds together in a single field all the traces by which the written text is constituted. (76)

Were a text to self-consciously emphasize (for it could be argued that *all* texts exemplify Barthes' idea) this model outlined by Barthes, it might reflect a random collection of stories, an inventory of competing discourses, or a fragmentation of narrative form to the point of a dissolution of the plot, as do DeLillo, Lessing, and Acker. Formally, one could indeed trace narrative fragmentation as a means of discovering the "traces by which the written text is constituted." However, *Almanac of the Dead* complicates such a reading since Silko insists on the preservation of stories and storytelling as political activism. In this chapter I will be charting narrative fragmentation in Silko's novel as a discursive practice that emphasizes the multiplication of voice and meaning and the preservation of Native American culture. For the purposes of this discussion I am defining fragmentation as the division of narrative development into random pieces and the breaking down of any autonomous main character into a stream of many voices and stories. Silko's specific use of narrative fragmentation results in a novel of resistance fundamentally different from the Western literary canon and from postmodernism, as I will show. In order to focus my discussion, for the most part I have limited my scope to two sections of the novel, part five, "The Fifth World," and part six, "One World, Many Tribes," because these sections carry the main representational thrust of the novel, the preservation of ancient storytelling.

As one might suspect, critics tend to disagree on the nature of Silko's resistance. What elicits adjectives like "vengeful" in describing this novel are the ways in which Silko relentlessly represents capitalism as economic violence, and in particular, her insistence that economic violence against displaced indigenous peoples is always war. There are historically recognizable wars going on in this novel—old conquests and genocides, WWI, WWII and Vietnam, Central America, but there are also invisible, economically determined wars given voice, such as drug wars, race wars, sex wars, wars on crime, wars on poverty, wars on homelessness, even psychic warfare. It is as if Silko sets a calendar of Western wars down only to interrupt them with more subtle, because repressed, warfare. The forms that invade the story—and I use the word "invade" because there is a structural attack underway—come from a variety of forces. The novel is informed as much by Native American myth as by U.S. history, class struggle, race wars, capitalism and above all, a violence that saturates every sphere of human life. In the clash between Native

American and U.S. histories, the narrative itself breaks into fragments, converging discourses, and conflicting languages. The flattening of history into a set of twisting times and crossing discourses, the fragmentation of characters, the pulverization of a culture saturated by war—all these characterize the 763 pages of Leslie Silko's *Almanac of the Dead*. Again, on the surface, the novel seems to be not only an example of the relationship between war and the literary postmodern, but perhaps a quintessential example, because *Almanac*, in its narrative structure and its thematic play, does appear to stage a system of codes, images, maps, stories and fragments with which we are asked to navigate.

One answer comes from Silko herself, who, in a review of Louise Erdrich's novel *The Beet Queen*, characterized her writing as the result of "academic, postmodern, so-called experimental influences" in direct tension with Native American oral tradition. According to Silko, the postmodern literary aesthetic is the product of the fragmentation of contemporary society as portrayed by the alienated Western writer and as mediated by and through language (Silko, "Artifact," 178-9). The tail end of the review takes a much harsher turn, however, when Silko charges Erdrich with failing to preserve native traditions:

> *The Beet Queen* is a strange artifact, an eloquent example of the political climate in America in 1986. It belongs on the shelf next to the latest report from the United States Civil Rights Commission, which says black men have made tremendous gains in employment and salary. This is the same shelf that holds *The Collected Thoughts of Edwin Meese on First Amendment Rights* and Grimm's *Fairy Tales*. (179)

Silko is particularly critical of Erdrich on the issue of narrative form, claiming that a radical Native American aesthetic would reflect the ontological landscape in which many Native Americans exist in the past and in the present, a landscape where competing realities as well as an invasion of Pueblo land and spiritual realms by occupying forces emerged. In other words, Silko is calling for a fundamentally different kind of move than the representation of the fragmentation of contemporary society in which the alienated Western writer's only link to other humans and spirituality is through language. In a way, she is calling for an artistic practice that participates in race, class and property struggles, an idea I will return to later.

Other critics respectfully diverge from this idea. For instance, Pérez Castillo points out how snugly Silko's work buffets Brian McHale's definition of postmodern representation, in which he claims that texts emerge not as passive mirrors of reality but as a place where two or more worlds battle for supremacy. According to McHale, unlike modernist texts, where the impulse to master a chaotic universe most often characterized by the white male European subject was emphasized, in the postmodern text, an aesthetic of discontinuity, heteroglossia, and difference emerges. Similarly, in the book

Recovering the Word, Essays on Native American Literature, Brian Swann and Arnold Krupat inventory the ways in which Native American literature both resists and participates in the movements of the dominant culture surrounding it. Edith Swan has shown how Silko, as well versed in Marx and Freud as she is Pueblo myth, often makes use of psychoanalytic theory, deconstruction, and critical theory as "stories" that alternately inform and invade the stories of Native peoples, and Paula Gunn Allen traced the influence of Freud's texts on Silko in "The Psychological Landscape of *Ceremony.*" However, Allen in particular has continued to argue for a violent distinction between Silko's narrative strategies and postmodernism. In a comment from "Special Problems in Teaching Leslie Marmon Silko's *Ceremony*," Allen puts the idea in very violent terms, claiming that she could no more "do (or sanction) the kind of ceremonial investigation of *Ceremony* done by some researchers than I could slit my mother's throat" (381).

One question that emerges then would be how do we locate a text or set of texts that would serve as a good model for contrast in literary history? Because oral literature is performative, written texts of oral expression can present only one dimension of a pluralistic experience. For example, in a tradition where an intense interactive context is built up, extending as it does into a tradition of previous performances and shared cultural references, a whole world of aesthetic norms and cutlural expectations unique to Native Americans or to a specific tribe or group would necessarily hinder the reading of any particular text. The verbal event of oral tradition already challenges the form of the novel, since song, storytelling, dance, performance, religious expression, vision quests, and prayer are not "textual" experiences in the way that novelistic narrative is. One might argue then that the best context within which to approach a text such as Silko's would be a historical and ethnographic one, in which case texts such as *The Experience of Five Christian Indians: Or, the Indian's Looking Glass for the White Men* (1833), *Black Hawk: An Autobiography* (1955), *Our Ancestors: Tlingit Oral Narratives* (1987), *The Voice in the Margin: Native American Literature and the Canon* (1989) or perhaps an annual report of the Bureau of American Ethnology would serve. However, Silko's text carries ghostly echoes from each of these texts, suggesting that none of them might stand as a stable model of contrast, and lending evidence to the notion that her narrative strategy engages postmodern formal turns.

Two of the key formal features which Silko self consciously interrupts are narrative time and narrative development. Silko lets go of the narrator altogether and represents time as random: "The old ones did not believe the passage of years caused old age. They had not believed in the passage of time at all" (19). In a section of the book titled "Fragments From the Ancient Notebooks," Silko represents past and present, reality and narrative as fundamentally unstable:

A day began at sunset. "Reality" was variously defined or described.

Narrative as analogue for the actual experience, which no longer exists; a mosaic of memory and imagination. (570)

In other words, Silko's novel represents the very terms of formal experiment that realist and modernist, perhaps even postmodernist writers addressed, as "reality." The nature of Silko's world is that these forms were always unstable. According to Silko, that instability is timeless and narrative form is a metaphor for that instability.

In terms of narrative development, Silko employs perpetual narrative fragmentation. *Almanac* turns the genre of the war novel on its head in many of the same formal ways that Heinemann, DeLillo, Lessing and Acker do. What makes Silko's use of fragmentation so different, however, is her emphasis on an arena of geographic, and by extension, spiritual suffering.

Almanac of the Dead charts a history of America as *one* of the Americas from the point of view of colonized and dispossessed indigenous peoples. The novel is divided into six parts that prioritize the history of the land over the history of events: "The United States of America," "Mexico," "Africa," "The Americas," "The Fifth World," and "One World, Many Tribes." As I mentioned earlier, main characters in the novel dissolve, however, a few main "figures" emerge: Seese, a character spinning around in a double world made up of the centrifugal force of drugs, money and violence on the one hand and Native American tradition on the other; Yoeme, a Yaqui woman who escaped execution in 1918 and who leaves the almanac to her granddaughters Lecha and Zeta; Lecha, an ex-talk show psychic who is transcribing and translating the historic notebooks of her people; Lecha's sister Zeta, a "matriarch" of an Arizona ranch. To this list I would add the land, a territory which records and responds to the warring impulses of its inhabitants and its invaders; history, a series of dead fragments emerging and disappearing like a text continually lost and found; and the almanac itself, a book made up of plagiarism, stolen forgeries, copies, myths and faithfully recorded oral traditions, penned by half crazy half revolutionary keepers and guardians over the ages.

A general trajectory for reading then becomes how does one read geographic suffering and history in the forms that Silko provides us. She seems to carry the ghost of marxist ideology throughout the *Almanac*. I say that because race, class, and property rights struggles are issues that shape nearly all the characters in the book. At issue is how to read those stories, and the answer given in the almanac is, as "dead matter." History and the oral stories of the past are quite often referred to as dead (569; 571; 573; 579-80). To further complicate reading, Silko insists that this dead matter must be understood by its readers as fertile information, or history is lost. While the almanac is said to have "living power within it, a power that would bring all tribal people of the Americas together to retake the land" (569), it is also described as an accumulation of "fragments that had been debris" (569).

But how does one read "debris," "death," "ruin" and narrative fragmentation as generative of anything? Silko's answer seems to be in the relationship between the past and the present: "The image of a memory exists in the present moment" (575). In the past, Native American myth and ritual inscribed identity and culture: "The old stories lived alongside people; they had shape and voice as brothers and sisters" (350). In the present, economy, and in particular, capitalism, inscribes identity and culture. The discovery of America is described as violence through robbery: "A beginning of vexation, a beginning of robbery with violence" (576). World war begins between 1500 and 1600, the years in which the "great war" and plague begin to spread, described in jarringly economic terms: "Lawsuits descend, taxes and tribute descend" (578). In other words, if we remember our history lessons, the riches seized by Hernando Cortés (1519 to 1521) and Francisco Pizarro (1533) translated into "world war," in economic and cultural terms, for the Aztec and Inca empires. Similar to but not the same as Acker's Empire, in Silko's history lesson, economic expansion is synonymous with a neverending world war.

A significant discussion of capitalism and aesthetics that intersects Silko comes from Walter Benjamin. While it is true enough that Benjamin inhabited a different historical moment than Silko does (the mid-1930s), both authors share similar views: history is a narrative of violence that can be traced from the position of the exile, capitalism generates productive forces that make its abolition both possible and necessary, and history contains repressed material that we must learn to read against the grain, as a form of resistance. Furthermore, the "guardians" of history in *Almanac*, like Benjamin's historical materialist, are charged with finding and recording the fragments of history before they disappear. According to Benjamin in his "Theses on the Philosophy of History," the past "can be seized only as an image which flashes up at the instant when it can be recognized and is never seen again."[1] The job of the historical materialist, in Benjamin's terms, is to "seize hold of a memory as it flashes up at a moment of danger" (255). The stakes were very high and the danger very immediate in war-torn Europe:

> The danger affects both the content of the tradition and its receivers. The same threat hangs over both: that of becoming a tool of the ruling classes. In every era the attempt must be made anew to wrest tradition away from a conformism that is about to overpower it. (255)

The critical task that Benjamin called for, to brush history "against the grain," by excavating the "ruins" of man, is the same kind of reading that Silko's novel emphasizes: "Only fragments of the original pages remained" (570); "Without the almanac, the people would not be able to recognize the days and months yet to come, days and months that would see the people retake their land" (570). In each case the authors are asking readers to redefine history, to see it differently than it has been presented thus far, an activity that Benjamin describes as an allegorical way of seeing:

Narrative Fragmentation 105

In allegory the observer is confronted with the *facies hippocratica* of history as a petrified, primordial landscape. Everything about history that, from the very beginning, had been untimely, sorrowful, unsuccessful, is expressed in a face—or rather a death's head. And although such a thing lacks all 'symbolic' freedom of expression, all classical proportion, all humanity, nevertheless, this is the form in which man's subjection to nature is most obvious and it significantly gives rise to not only the enigmatic question of the nature of human existence as such, but also of the biographical historicity of the individual. This is the allegorical way of seeing.[2]

For Benjamin, the cultural productions of man are absorbed in a "petrified, primordial landscape" made up of an endless pile of fragments in which all of human history is figured. Similarly, for Silko, a dead landscape exists that is reflected in the almanac: "Dead souls live with us, but they don't break the silence" (604). According to Silko, one must learn to "interpret the messages sent in other, dead languages" (604). What emerges from juxtaposing these two texts and authors is an argument for reading their works as a landscape, a ruin, a site, and formally speaking, both give us such a place to read, Benjamin in his "Theses on the Philosophy of History," a set of narrative and allegorical fragments, and Silko in *Almanac*. Which is to say that both use artistic practice to engage the reader in active participation in class struggle. Put slightly differently, both present us with the text as a site, a dead landscape where writing and reading are political acts.

I do not mean to conflate Europe in the 1930s with Native American experience or Benjamin with Silko. But neither can one ignore the plea both make in the name of what passes for historical record. And in the end I find that Benjamin's exile lends legitimacy to my connections. In other words, I find exile and occupation and dispossesion to be inter-related terms and experiences common to resistance literature. For Silko in particular, to read history against the grain means reading representations of drug wars, security strategies, capitalism and the economic organization of indigenous peoples against their subtexts: the resistance of land, of history, of bodies, Native American myth and story, environmentalist and Native American coalitions, water rights accounts, eco-techno-terrorisms, inner city riots, and the takeover of land by indigenous majorities. Silko's novel carries the echo of Benjamin's warning: *"even the dead* will not be safe from the enemy if he wins. And this enemy has not ceased to be victorious" (255). The genocide of Europe shares a frightening link with quieter (because repressed, denied) genocide: Native American. Only the features of the war have shifted. The most important question Silko raises, like Benjamin's, is can we recognize the past in the present or not, can the stories speak through the history?

The title of this novel points to the backward and forward movement of the future and the past as they continually interrupt each other. The *prediction* for the future is alive in the present. An allegorical reading of the novel would suggest that we read history against itself by sifting through its "ruins." As Silko represents it, "the white man hated to hear anything about spirits because spirits were already dead and could not be tortured and butchered or shot" (581). The most important way in which *Almanac* presents a formal alternative to a Western version of the history of America is through fragmented stories. Through the recording of a different record, through codes, glyphs, and fragments, through transcriptions, translations, plagiarisms, stolen forgeries, copies and an oral tradition painstakingly "rendered," or, through representing history as a site of ruin, some stories are preserved in the wake of history. At issue is what stories can do:

> Yoeme's story of her deliverance changed forever the odds against all captives; each time a revolutionist escaped death in one century, two revolutionists escaped certain death in the following century even if they never heard such an escape story. Where such miraculous escape stories are greatly prized and rapidly circulated, miraculous escapes from death gradually increase. (581)

One thing that stories can do is change, reorganize, resist and defy the history of a culture based on the conquest of people and land. This is one place where Silko diverges from a marxist trajectory. Where Benjamin argued for the revolutionary possibility in the newly emerging artistic practices of reproduction, particularly mechanical reproduction, Silko's interpretation of reproduction is not mechanical.[3] It is linguistic, spiritual, and oral; revolutionary possibility and resistance to occupying forces comes from multiplying stories. For instance, the truth of Silko's story, its authenticity, its authority, is completely subordinated to the idea that the reader must understand that narrative is unstable, fragmented and changing, and that it *changes and reproduces voices and authors,* as the almanac promises:

> One day a story will arrive in your town. There will always be disagreement over direction—whether the story came from the southwest or the southeast. The story may arrive with a stranger, a traveler thrown out of his home or country months ago. Or the story may be brought by an old friend, perhaps a parrot trader. But after you hear the story, you and the others prepare by the new moon to rise up against the slave masters. (578)

Again the unstable nature of the story and the teller are emphasized, and the crisis in interpretation for the reader is included in that formal emphasis, as if to perform Barthes' point at Benjamin's site. *Almanac of the Dead* truly represents a set of fragmented stories under the belly of history, pieces of lives and images left from one generation to the next to be re-excavated and recognized by the present *in a material sense.* Like Barthes' claim, in which the work of art reflects its own "fundamental illegibility," *Almanac* places the arena of struggle in the reader. Like Benjamin's claims about history and artistic production, *Almanac* superimposes the inevitable erosion of history onto

Narrative Fragmentation

the erosion of narrative meaning. Benjamin's "allegorical way of seeing" would seem to come into play here. But unlike Barthes and Benjamin, Silko seems to be saying that discursive practices such as storytelling still have something to show us even as capitalism has progressed. I think Silko would be a good reader of Benjamin in this case, for she would read Benjamin's form, the narrative mode and narrative fragments in "Theses," for example, as a vehicle for knowledge.[4] For Silko then, a story is a form of resistance.

To illustrate this distinction, let me offer some examples of what else a dead story can do. In a passage concerning Geronimo, Silko isolates the stakes involved in two kinds of stories that are in conflict with one another through a tale told by the ancient woman Yoeme:

> ... But the Apache man identified in the photographs is not, of course, the man the U.S. army has been chasing. He is a man who always agreed to play the role for the protection of the other man. The man in the photographs had been promised safe conduct by the man he protected. The man in the photographs was a brilliant and resourceful man. He may not have known that while he he would find wealth and fame in the lifelong captivity, he would not again see the mountains during his lifetime. The man who fled had further work to do, work that could not be done in captivity. (129)

One man splits in two in this story. While the American historical version of Geronimo lives on finding "wealth and fame in lifelong captivity" and helping to sustain an American version of history in which the Indian needed to be colonized, another man, and with him another story, escapes. He flees because he has "further work to do," because he sustains a different story, a hidden story. The other man moves on into a myth which becomes one thread in a larger story of Native American history. This "other man" came to Yoeme during a time of great danger. She watches him disappear into "a gull riding a wave," and recognizes immediately that he is a carrier of stories. This "split" is a crisis in interpretation. What dead stories can do is multiply meanings. But which meanings are we meant to follow? My argument that we read allegorically hits a limit here: whose allegory? Discursive systems, as Foucault argued, authorize some representations and not others. Would Benjamin have us read the image of Geronimo as he reads Klee's angel, as history? Would Silko?

To begin one must first remember that land is a character in this novel, and this is a major distinction between marxist and postmodernist theories and Silko's narrative strategies. For Silko, the land breathes, speaks, fights, loves, lives, dies and is reborn. It is like the skin of history, recording the movement of one culture against another in plagues, earthquakes, droughts, famines, and wars like bruises, wounds, and sutures. Based on an oral tradition, Silko's fiction, the land, the tribe, and the fate of any individual are inextricably linked. As Silko writes in the essay "Landscape, History, and the Pueblo Imagination," the ancients never conceived of removing themselves from the earth and sky, and human consciousness is in part located within the hills, canyons, cliffs, and the plants, linked to a matrilineal set of clan ties. According to Silko, since the relationship that Native American people have to the land is radically different from European or Anglo American versions, neither marxism's nor postmodernism's literary forms can possibly account for the ways in which the Native American subject is alienated—through genocide, through slavery, through a dispersal of families and individuals through economic oppression, invasion and war (though one could make the argument that Engels and Levi-Srauss intersect the discussion here). According to Silko, dispossession brought about alienation from the land and from the realm of spirits, the most damaging form of disempowerment for native peoples, distinct from the European alienation represented through modernist and postmodernist forms.

The alienation of man from his ancestral connection to the land and the spirit world is registered through storytelling. Storytelling forges a much different version of history and time, and by extension, narrative form. In some passages the land and the body share eerily similar markings. Silko represents time according to land and bodies, rather than the chronological events or actions of man. For instance, the year 1560 is "The year of the plague—intense cold and fever—bleeding from nose and coughing, twisted necks and large sores erupt. Plague ravages the country side" (577). The year 1566: "between one and two in the afternoon an earthquake caused great destruction" (577). The year 1590 is represented in both geographic and anthropomorphized terms:

> On January 3, 1590, the epidemic began: cough, chills, and fever from which people died . . . the face of the moon was covered with darkness soon after sunset. It was really a great darkness and the moon could not be seen. The surface of the earth could not be seen at all. (577)

The almanac records time according to the land, not the events of man, by relentlessly referencing the land and the body in a close symbiotic relationship that reflects a cycle of life and decay: "The land of the dead is a land of flowers and abundant food" (573), a land where death, like stories, gives rise to continual new life, and where European and later American invasion—of land, bodies and stories—begins a war that does not end. "Twisted necks and large sores" are conflated with "ravaged countryside," earthquakes and coughs and chills are conflated with "the surface of the earth." What the land and the body have in common in *Almanac* is this: they exist in a condition of perpetual war, perpetual invasion, perpetual occupation. Thus the fundamental alienation in the novel is the separation of the land from the people and their stories.

Unlike other almanacs, *Almanac of the Dead* gives voice to corpses, ghosts, ravaged and invaded land. Earlier I said that Silko finds the revolutionary possibilities of art not in mechanical reproduction but in discursive

Narrative Fragmentation 109

forms of reproduction. Like language, the land records and organizes the chaos of experience. Like stories, the land gives meaning to the confusion of events and images. Like a character, the land registers psychic impulses and conflicts as well as their social equivalents, through earthquakes, droughts and famine. Each is a border of either violence or growth. Silko juxtaposes the history of U.S. economic control with stories of geographic suffering. At the level of novelistic language, then, land is eroding and suffering, and erosion and suffering are reflected in the fragmentation of character and story, discursive borders on which meaning hinges. How one reads the alienation of people from the land, alternately figured as the arena of struggle, the site of ruin, the skin of history, is therefore the most important issue in the book.

One example of the role that land plays as an arena of struggle and a site of ruin on which meaning hinges is Tucson, a kind of borderland between binaries—between peace and war, between high capitalism and Native American tradition, between north and south, between production and destruction, between disease and healing. Tucson represents a border between the U.S. of the past, the present, and the future. Tucson is variously represented in the novel as a commodity (661), a site of war (656), a site of sacred tradition (762), an allegory for Mexico (650; 661) a border between possibilities. A majority of the characters who emerge in the novel have some connection to Tucson: Leah Blue the real estate tycoon who sees Tucson as a Disney World where water can be bought and sold; Trigg who wants to build a U.S. plastic surgery center; Seese who sees Tucson as a territory for drug smuggling activities; Lecha, the talk show psychic whose duty it is to transcribe the notebooks and read the signs of the land, looks to Tucson as a territory one might read like geographic Braille. It is as if Silko has answered Conrad's question: we will take the manager's course, and make all cultures into markets.

But another story of Tucson is embedded inside each of these. What is in contrast to a variety of U.S. economic land use issues—from the formation of reservations to the discovery of oil to the battle over water rights—is the land itself. The almanac predicts that the forces of the earth will work in the service of Native Americans. Earthquakes, floods, and famines lead to "civil strife, civil crisis, civil war" (756), all chances for uprise or change. Storms "bruise" the land, and as I mentioned earlier, earthquakes and floods leave scars we might ordinarily associate with a human immune system under attack. The buying and selling of land always has a natural disaster close by. As Yoeme puts it, "The war was the same war it had always been" (631) and by that she means that plague, starvation and cholera are merely code names for invasion, occupation and starvation. Contemporary notions of "real estate" in this case are threatened by natural disaster in the service of indigenous people—houses do not just slide down the California hills or disappear into Southern floods for no reason; the ideologies that supported their foundation are under attack from the ground up.

By continually writing a different relationship between the land and people, between setting and character, Silko undoes the idea that a character inhabits a setting in the traditional sense. In this novel, the setting has subsumed the character, and with it the significance of any single character's actions. Again the echo of a postmodern reading presents itself. In postmodern terms, the setting has lost its power as an external descriptive device and merges into the work itself. In Native American terms, relationships to land have always already figured and disfigured the western convention of "setting" and "character," so it is not likely that her narrative strategies can be explained in exclusively postmodern terms. Rather, it is as if Silko is showing us what it would look like to follow Benjamin's call to read allegorically and showing us the blind spot of a such a reading as well. Such a reading would identify the importance of economic inscription between land and people, the possibilities for revolution, but miss the resistance narrative that the narrative forms—such as fragmentation—make available. To extend Harlow's argument, land *and* literary forms are arenas of struggle.

In order to tease out that point I would like to return to the notion of resistance, keeping in mind my claims about the narrative fragment. In *Resistance Literature*, Harlow shows how narratives of resistance compromise their own, historically specific genres and their specific narrative features. She argues that the historical dimensions of resistance movements are connected to the narratives in ways that we have yet to account for. I would like to extend her analysis of the resistance novel by charting such connections in Silko's *Almanac*, specifically at the level of character.

According to Harlow, novelistic narrative contains the possibility of resisting dominant ideologies. For example, the form of the novel provides a chance for disenfranchised writers from occupied territories to appropriate and challenge the historical and political "master narratives," the ideological paradigms that have dominated western literary tradition. The resistance narrative challenges the colonization narrative and the forms that serve to preserve and maintain dominant cultural paradigms.

Harlow identifies the ways in which narrative structures shift according to *specific* historical situations. For example, according to Harlow, the resistance novel seeks out different historical endings and these endings are already implicit, contained within the narrative analysis and construction of the conditions and problematic of the historical situation itself. She analyzes narratives of resistance generated out of South Africa, Lebanon, Israel, Palestine, El Salvador, and Nicaragua. Within the context of these narratives of resistance, *Almanac* can be understood as a text which engages and challenges "the dominant and hegemonic discourse of an occupying or colonizing power by attacking the symbolic foundations of that power and erecting symbolic structures of its own" (85). The dominant hegemonic discourses in Silko's novel concern property invasion and dispossession and the displacement of native peoples, and the *specific* forms resistance takes in Silko's novel are always figured by land and by borders. By looking next at Silko's treatment of character, one can chart how she develops a "border" subject position that reflects the site or arena of struggle that she makes of land and literary form.

Criticism of the novel has often centered on Silko's inattention to character development. Especially in contrast to perhaps her most famous character, Tayo, from *Ceremony*, the seventy or so "voices" which constitute *Almanac of the Dead* over a period of 500 years are, indeed, less developed. The danger one risks, as Silko explains, is that she is not drawing a human character and psyche in depth, but attempting to "give history a character." The character of history emerging from *Almanac of the Dead* is fragmented into a series of voices, figures from many different positions who remain "caught" in a position that borders on violence *as well as* the chance for resistance or identity. So the first place that Silko breaks down conventions of characterization is with her refusal to create any single authoratative voice, and the second is her constant multiplication of voice into a kind of endlessly mutable identity.

The thematic direction that the characters take is based on a metaphor of scattering:

> All Native American tribes had similar prophecies about the appearance, conflict with and eventual disappearance of things European. The almanacs had warned the people hundreds of years before the Europeans arrived. The people living in large towns were told to scatter, to disperse to make the murderous work of the invaders more difficult. (570)

Silko's formal narrative strategy is to scatter and disperse characters at the level of narrative language. Since the dominant hegemonic discourses in Silko's novel concern the displacement of native peoples and the dispossesion of land, this formal scattering and dispersal of character does not seem to be associated with the postmodern narrative impulses I have outlined in previous chapters. The cost of this narrative strategy is that no one character ever emerges as a central "structuring" device for the story. But the benefit of this strategy is that the characters can be used to expose something else, to stand in for something else. The task for the reader is to figure out what that "something else" might be.

One possibility involves Silko's claim about "giving history" a character. However, characters only ever surface in glimpses, making the analysis of them nearly impossible. In fact, it is as if their only appearances are determined by economic or violent causes. A real estate tycoon named Leah Blue has a secret, sexual rendezvous with a small time entrepreneur, Trigg, a man confined to a wheelchair. The lower half of Trigg's body doesn't work. As they have sex, or something like it with Leah riding Trigg's dead lower half, Leah dreams of a crystal city in the desert, Blue Water Development Company, and Trigg dreams of a sex mall and an international center for organ transplants in Tucson, two visions that show up again in slightly more detail throughout the novel. True to their culturally determined economic boundaries, each character embodies a force running through capitalist consumer culture. Their very identities, or more precisely, positions, since each identity rendered in the novel seems more like a position, match their fortune hunting—Trigg's physical, sexual and financial helplessness translates into dreams of luxury hospitals, plasma donor centers, substance abuse houses, and visions of making Tucson the health and beauty capital of the States. In contrast, Leah's future dream world reflects her bourgeois position by turning water and land into luxury commodities for the wealthy and beautiful: "The *others* had to live someplace; let it be Tucson"(662). Between them is dead love, a dead desert, half-alive bodies struggling to find economic identity *where a nation has failed to provide them with anything else*. In other words, these two characters point to the economic inscription of identity. This is all we ever learn about them. In this case, giving history a character translates into an economic representation or position.

While her characters remain underdeveloped in the traditional sense, and while they come and go within five pages, like most of the characters in *Almanac of the Dead*, what is represented is not a personal psychology but a series of "captured" identities where we might view, for example, the economic inscription of subjectivity. Leah has understood water as the oil of her time. Wealthy whites will want to escape from the barren and filthy desert of "those others." Trigg has understood a mass of human leftovers from the drug wars, the wars on crime, the war on homelessness and even the war on fat and ugliness as a vast well of profit. In this case individual psyches are translated into figures mirroring a society in progress, a society threatened by the effects of its economic overdetermination. And in effect, all the characters together in the novel produce a map for a social identity fragmented by economic inscription.

Another character marked by her economic inscription is Lecha, the character responsible for transcribing the almanac, arguably the most important "job" in the book:

> Back in Tucson Lecha had begun to make notes and sift through the piles of paper and old notebooks. Seese had been surprised when Lecha had skipped the late-afternoon and midnight shots of Demerol; Lecha no longer took Percodan at noon because she wanted to stay alert to decipher the old notebooks. (592)

An ex-talk show psychic, Lecha is not the conventional version of a novelistic visionary, but neither is she a postmodern subject. Lecha is where the visionary has gone, between the worlds of fragmented identities that carry only the traces of former traditions *and* the wounded world of economic systems of human exchange (drug culture, self-help, television), *and* Native American myth. In other words, caught between consumer culture, drug addiction and Native American tradition, she carries both the limits and the possibilities of vision. Her success or failure depends upon which collective

Narrative Fragmentation   113

discourse she listens to. The novel does not provide an answer to such a question. In place of knowing an answer we get an open questions mark: we never find out whether or not she translated the almanac material "properly." We only see a glimpse of her struggle.

But something else is going on with the characters' endless economic inscription. More often than not, in their short appearances, the reader finds instances where borders of identity are more important than individual characters. Identities often "hover" between consumer culture and native culture. Seese is another figure who surfaces sporadically in the novel. She is a survivor with a vengeance who makes her way in the world through drug deals and fast money. A real woman on the edge, one of Seese's functions in the novel is to represent a life in the drug culture and a corresponding representative drug bust scene. In the fragments in which she appears, we get the picture of an addict and of the economy of cocaine that drives the business of America's underworld. She is poor, Mexican, Indian, addicted and female, all codes for that with which we need to be at war with because it attacked us (war on drugs), that which we need to clean up because it is dirty (war on crime), that which threatens to devour the authority of the State (the alien feminine). Naturally, the cops are after her, but the drug bust turns out to have a sub-text: a set-up by the cops to kill an undercover cop who is not falling "in line" with the boys. After the bust, Seese is tied up and interrogated about the order of events. What happens in her scene is a multiplication of one story into two, not unlike the duplicating Geronimo story:

> Then Seese knew. The dead cop had been set up by his own people. Cops took care of their own kind if they stepped out of line. They had kept asking her if she was sure the undercover man had come in the door first because the department had certain guidelines and procedures . . . Uniformed officers broke through the doors first; undercover followed. . . Seese got the picture. (698)

In other words, Seese sees a different story wherein a different kind of addict surfaces, the cop who kills his own in order to preserve a certain version of male power and fraternity. That second sight allows her to uncover a subtext, that is, in the symbolic hierarchy of law and order, the police are addicts with power: "The police needed to be controlled because they are too easily addicted to torturing people"(649). In this case, to "get the picture" means to read for the story underneath the surface. Where the western story of the dangerous, drug smuggling Mexican surfaces, a second story of the symbolic fraternal order needing to destroy one of its own is also exposed.

Two stories sit atop one another: two addicts—the drug addict racially and economically coded (Mexican and poor), and the cop addict legislator of law also racially and economically coded (white, male and middle class). The cops kill the criminal, the "criminal" is a cop, the fictionalized race-identified criminal—Seese—escapes incarceration because "cocaine smuggling was a lesser evil than a breach in the security of the white male power structure" (650). In other words, the stereotypical story of the Mexican drug smuggler and the white police officer enforcing the war on drugs is underwritten by an ordinarily repressed story, the story of male fraternity that supports a certain version of culture's symbolic authority. One story is embedded inside another, one war is embedded inside another. By exposing a hidden story of the dominant culture's addiction to power inside the story of a police arrest for drug dealing, Silko shows in discursive terms how prohibitions against breaking the law are predicated on, and cover over, a fear that the inside/outside border between cop and criminal will collapse.

There is yet a further complication to this scene. The young undercover cop who gets killed in the drug bust scene is the lover of Ferro, Lecha's homosexual son. Silko uses the border of sexuality as both a limit and a possibility. The story of Ferro's homosexual love for a blue eyed, blonde haired undercover cop is juxtaposed to the perversion of fraternity and camaraderie, or the homoerotic desire, of the cops themselves. For example, the Thursday Club is an elite brotherhood made up of law enforcement officers, judges, lawyers and high ranking police officers in Tucson. Silko takes the notion of the "old boy's network" to its sexual extreme:

> The Thursday Club hired pretty Mexican boys to chop wood bare chested all winter while club members watched them from the sun-room as they sat in chaise lounges sipping cocktails or sucking on small oranges. (644)

The cops kill the blonde undercover cop because he would not "stay in line." He dared to fall in love with an "outsider," one of the dangerous others. The very force that defines their power is also that which is most overtly condemned as disgusting and immoral when it leaks out beyond the borders of that power. Homoeroticism that is not contained by the power structure becomes a threat to its order and a mirror of its own dangerous interiority. Silko seems to suggest that homoeroticism as the temptation to stray—stray as in unconfined by the power structure—is a wound in need of suture from the point of view of the dominant race and class. By exposing a hidden story of homoerotic desire in the dominant culture's power structures, Silko again shows in discursive terms how prohibitions, in this case against homoerotic desire, are predicated on, and cover over, a fear that the borders between meanings will collapse. In other words, there is an unstable border between Fero's homosexual love story and the cops' homoeroticism, illuminated in Silko's juxtaposition of the stories on top of one another. The duplication of stories is endless, no single story ever dominates.

Like the criminal and sexual stereotypes deployed and atomized in the novel, racial stereotypes of all sorts are built and undone in *Almanac*. A clearly racist character appears in the novel for a short scene in a very unusual way. On a bus filled with upper class Mexicans and Central Americans traveling to the U.S., we meet Alegría. This character represents a non-stereotypical, at least from a white point of view, version of the "flight" to the U.S. from Mexico. In her ten-page journey from the civil unrest of Mexico to the safety of the U.S. bourgeois haven, she is robbed and abandoned in the desert along with the other passengers on the "luxury bus tour." Her survival in the heat depends on three things: her ability to define herself against the lower class "others," her ability to safeguard the pouch of gems she is carrying, and her ability to decide whether or not she can drink her own urine in order to survive.

Alegría's views are violently conservative: "the poor are born to suffer"(668). She defines herself by her class and against the other passengers: "Alegría was sad for Mexico, but she had watched Bartolomeo and the Marxists struggle to teach the people and it was hopeless; there was nothing to be done. The masses were naturally lazy everywhere, and they often starved; that was their nature"(671). In her "survival of the fittest" economic journey, she analyzes the corpses of those who do not survive in direct relation to her own success:

> Alegría felt euphoric each time she passed another corpse. Guatemalans and Hondurans seemed to die in twos and threes; the Mexicans dropped like flies, one by one, alone. She had lost count, but she knew the "secret system": each corpse she passed advanced Alegría closer to safety. The more the others died, the more likely it was that [she] would be saved; that was only simple mathematics. (676)

Alegría reads the field of corpses the way white culture does, as the advancement of civilization. When she is finally rescued by gun and refugee runners (two Mexican women named Liria and Sarita and a group of Catholic priests and nuns), we discover she is blonde. In other words, it takes her rescue for us to find this out. Two of her Mexican saviors think: "It must be the *coyotes* now were crossing a higher class of people as the civil wars in the South worsened" (678). The "flight" of the blonde white woman from the South to the North, and her subsequent "rescue" by gun and refugee runners who cross back and forth across the border ruptures the U.S./Mexican, citizen/illegal alien dichotomy. This is no simple inversion in which white people are suddenly bad and brown people are suddenly good. The white woman is recoded as "alien" and "foreign," and the Mexican women are recoded as the "rescuers" and "preservers" of that alien and foreign status. They move back and forth across a geographic border trafficking both guns and identities.

Furthermore, the gun-runners are a fairly ambiguous pair; it is difficult to determine whose side they are on. That is because in the war that Silko arranges, it does not matter. Because I have argued that Silko's landscape is perpetual war, one might expect to find characters who are soldiers in that war. But there are no soldiers nor armies per se in the novel—the soldiers are dead, and the armies are ghosts of Lakota warriors. Instead there are symbolic figures of Western power and authority, such as policemen, judges and tax collectors, and figures of resistance, such as terrorists, thieves, drug smugglers and con-artists. The economic organization of civilian society has translated soldiers and their enemies into a landscape where the homeless and sick, the addict and the criminal, now lumped together by class with Mexican and Indian border populations, threaten to overwhelm and invade the sanctity of the white middle class. The new "enemy" of the State is its own people.

As if to underscore this version of war-as-fear, a vivid example of a minority terrorist who takes over a television station brings war back to an allegorical image. A figure of resistance, La Escapía, or, "The Meat Hook as she called herself" (590), has been trained by Cuban Marxists to help lead an all-tribal army. In a pirated television message La Escapía threatens to eat her enemies alive:

> La Escapía's big Indian face had filled the whole video screen. Her big Indian teeth flashed in the close-up. She said she chose the name La Escapía for battle because she thought it was hilarious. Hilarious how terrified the whites were of Indian wars. To further terrorize army and police officers, La Escapía promised if she captured high-ranking officers in battle, she would feed them the steel of her namesake and cook their testicles for lunch. (590)

As a good terrorist (recall Lessing, Acker, Fanon), La Escapía's "big Indian face" filling the screen is one of white America's worst nightmares. The uncontrollable other to excess, she represents everything the masculine, "secure" and "ordered" nation tries to define itself against. Transported via video image to local government video stations, The Meat Hook is resistance live and in color, invading white power through the air waves and winning by virtue of her excessive representability. One of the best bombs a disenfranchised, dispossessed, and brutalized culture has is the image of itself, a representation that its oppressors cannot face: the return of the creation come back to kill them. Arguably an example of the devouring feminine, the face "filled the whole video screen" in a "close-up" that flashes her "big Indian teeth." If we were to read the face allegorically, in Benjamin's terms, it is possible that a second story might emerge. In that story, her face subordinates her threat to white viewers to the meaning of the mode of production. Put slightly differently, it is the video image that takes primacy over the war-as-fear story; her face can be endlessly moved and repeated, her story of eating high-ranking officers can be endlessly moved and repeated, her identity endlessly moved and repeated.

The image of the face is a kind of border where identity is caught unfinished, neither dissolved nor constituted. Clearly this formal strategy shares some features with the disjunctions characteristic of the postmodern crisis in subjectivity and historicity. But for Silko, these postmodern theoretical explanations do not fully account for the experience of Native Americans. While postmodernity as an effect of economic globalization and information modes of production may match specific impacts on Native Americans, postmodern theoretical models, with their reliance of Western models of thought, do not. In particular, the critique of subjectivity and historicity characteristic of postmodern theoretical explanations is both engaged and challenged in Silko's novel. In *Almanac,* history is variously described as "vexation" (576); "an alien invasion" (577); "an epidemic" (577); "a revolution against slave masters" (578); media pimping (599); an addiction to electricity and technology (599); and camera love (617), and subjectivity is nowhere constituted that it does not illuminate a border where stories and interpretations multiply. It would seem that history and subjectivity are being called into question in postmodern terms.

However, how we articulate that notion depends upon what cultural, individual, and historic "positions" we occupy. In *Borderlands/La Frontera: The New Mestiza,* the critic and activist Gloria Anzaldúa provides a model of subjectivity in the figure of the "mestiza." Drawing from the work of Jose Vasconcelos, Anzaldúa theorizes a subject position predicated on "crossing over," or a "mixture of races" that provides a "hybrid progeny, a mutable, more malleable species with a rich gene pool" (78). From this hybridization she theorizes a "racial, ideological, cultural and biological cross-pollination, an "alien" consciousness" and a "new *mestiza* consciousness" that she terms a "consciousness of the Borderlands" (77). But this new position is not without struggle and danger: "The new mestiza's dual or multiple personality is plagued by psychic restlessness" (78). It is a restlessness characterized by a haunting question:

> Being tricultural, monolingual, bilingual, or multilingual, speaking a patois, and in a state of perpetual transition, the *mestiza* faces the dilemma of the mixed breed: which collectivity does the daughter of a darkskinned mother listen to? (78)

Therein rests the problem, albeit uncomfortably, to which Silko gives voice in her fragmented characterizations. According to Anzaldúa, at the borderland of identity, "commonly held beliefs of the white culture attack commonly held beliefs of the Mexican culture, and both attack commonly held beliefs of the indigenous culture" (87). For Anzaldúa this is both a dangerous and a productive site of resistance. By "standing on the opposite river bank" of white patriarchal oppression the oppressed gain a step toward cultural liberation, but because this relationship remains rooted in an oppressor/oppressed dynamic, this "counterstance locks one into a duel" (78). What she offers instead is a story in which these two "mortal combatants" are replaced by a psychic territory of crossing. This position is spatial, and available as an option to individuals as well as groups, reflected in the metaphor of the riverbank. Silko's novel provides formal provisional positions from which to view resistance as a philosophy of "crossing borders" (613).

For Anzaldúa, the first step of the mestiza is to "take an inventory" and to ask, "Just what did she inherit from her ancestors?" She must put history through a sieve in order to find her stories, and she must experience a conscious rupture between cultures. The mestiza "communicates that rupture, documents the struggle" (82). Silko's version is the almanac in which an inventory is taken of what might yet be inherited by native peoples and her answer seems to be language, or a resistance through discursive means, through stories that are arbitrary, changing, authorless, mutable, as chaotic as language itself.

Like the "new mestiza" described by Anzaldúa, the characters, whose stories are embedded within other stories, are scattered throughout the novel. Each character represents a border where conflict and resistance are equally available instead of set in opposition. Each character also represents a small, micro-instance that stages the costs and benefits of keeping borders rigid or making them flexible. And like the "new mestiza," each character, with differing degrees of success and failure, must develop a way to cope with personal and cultural contradictions. We never find out how a single character "resolves" those contradictions and ambiguities. Instead we see a freeze frame that locates the place where difference and change *might* be figured. One of the final images in the novel is that of a giant stone snake that "opens ancient history up" in the present: "The snake was looking south, in the direction from which the twin brothers and the people would come" (763). The snake's jaw is open wide, and on the ground near its head "was littered bits of turquoise coral, and mother-of-pearl" (761). Anzaldúa describes such a position and identity in psychic terms in *Borderlands/La Frontera:*

> We are the people who leap in the dark, we are the people on the knees of gods. In our very flesh, (r)evolution works out the clash of cultures. It makes us crazy constantly, but if the center holds, we've made some kind of evolutionary step forward. *Nuestra alma el trabajo,* the opus, the great alchemical work; spiritual *mestizaje,* a "morphongenesis," an inevitable unfolding. We have become the quickening serpent movement. (81)

One is reminded of Benjamin's reading of the angel of history in "Theses on the Philosophy of History," with "his mouth wide open" and his face turned away: "His face [is] turned toward the past. Where we perceive a chain of events, he sees one single catastrophe which keeps piling wreckage upon wreckage" (257). The last character to face the image in Silko's novel is left to interpret the snake, and he does not come to the same conclusion that Benjamin does. Where Benjamin identifies the danger of "the storm of progress," Silko leaves us in a different arena or territory: "The snake didn't care about uranium . . . Burned, radioactive, with all humans dead, the earth would still be sacred. Man was too insignificant to desecrate her" (762): Anzaldúa's quickening serpent, an inevitable unfolding. Even with humans gone, resistance retains importance; the land would be liberated from its oppressive state of property. Far from simply functioning as a gesture of the literary postmodern aesthetic, Silko's fragmentation is tied directly to geographic and spiritual dispossessions, to economic divisions, to cultures made up of exiles, features tied to the social situation of Native American history. The speaking subject is not only multiple, but resisting.

In a way, Silko provides an answer to a question posed by Fredric Jameson: can there be a form that resists the debilitating effects of postmodern culture? Perhaps Silko is writing a lesson about our current postmodern moment. In one scenario, the results are all-out war, with the white race being forced back to Europe and the indigenous people of America retaking the land. In another, in an imagined memory, one world with many tribes emerges, because the stories underneath the ones we tell ourselves about capitalism are read rather than repressed. In one sense, these stories are like Benjamin's ruins. But Benjamin's ruins do not fit Silko's text if we think about the land, rather than economy, inscribing identity. In her text, retaking the land is not an issue of property rights or a Marxist political trajectory. Retaking the land would mean understanding the story of capitalism as the definition of war.

NOTES

1. Walter Benjamin, *Illuminations*, Trans. Harry Zohn(New York: Schocken Books, 1969), p. 256.

2. Walter Benjamin, *The Origin of German Tragic Drama*, trans. John Osborne (London: NLB, 1977), 183-84.

3. In particular, two of Benjamin's essays, "The Author as Producer" and "The Work of Art in the Age of Mechanical Reproduction" promote the idea that there are revolutionary tendencies in art to be excavated from the production relations of capitalism. According to Benjamin, the productive forces in art include the artist and the artistic technique, especially reproductive techniques such as film and photography.

4. I am speaking in particular here of Benjamin's works such as "Unpacking my Library," "The Task of the Translator," "The Storyteller," and "Theses on the Philosophy of History." In "Theses" Benjamin makes specific formal use of the narrative mode as a form capable of representing his allegorical way of seeing, for example, in Theses IX.

CHAPTER VII
Conclusion: The Writing of War

WAR HAS BEEN REMEMBERED, CONVENTIONALIZED, MYTHOLOGIZED AND HISTORICAL-
ly charted in large part by literary means. Critical analysis of that literature has provided us with a means by which to read ourselves. One of the critical contexts of this study is charted in Paul Fussell's collection of the war literature of this century, *The Great War and Modern Memory*, in which he argues that "war as a historical experience [has] conspicuous imaginative and artistic meaning" (x). Beyond that argument, critics have tried to map out how it is that war and artistic production evolve in relation to one another in a variety of ways. In the introduction to this study I cited Robert Hughes' notion that war puts a pressure on art. Like Hughes, Andreas Huyssen argues in *After the Great Divide* that the period before 1960 produced a unique pressure of totalitarian control over all culture:

> The age of Hitler, Stalin, and the Cold War produced specific accounts of modernism . . . whose aesthetic categories cannot be totally divorced from the pressures of that era. (197)

According to Huyssen, that pressure produced a variety of artistic defensive strategies that led to the development of a Western codification of modernism as a canon of the twentieth-century. However, as Huyssen argues, in America, sometime between 1960 and 1970 a whole series of fundamental assumptions of the preceding decade fell away or changed; World War and the Cold War faded as the dominant pressures on art, and in their place came a war that challenged us to redefine ourselves and the stories we tell ourselves about war—the long and painful interval of the Vietnam war. Vietnam forged a unique relation between war and representation that we will never forget. It was the first war famous in part for "coming into our living rooms." Television will forever help to periodize that war. According to Huyssen,

Vietnam and mass technology emerged in a kind of symbiotic relationship that left us with unique pressures on artistic form:

> The situation in the 1970s seemed to be characterized by an ever wider dispersal and dissemination of artistic practices all working out of the ruins of the modernist edifice, raiding it for ideas, plundering its vocabulary and supplementing it with randomly chosen images and motifs from pre-modern and non-modern cultures as well as from contemporary mass culture. (196)

Ordinarily these changes are charted either historically or through aesthetic categories such as modernism or postmodernism. I am arguing that the stylistic and substantive changes in the novels of my study are not limited to the literary categories of modernism or postmodernism per se, but rather belong to a set of ongoing social and economic discourses of which the novel is a part. The definition of war is no longer understood by exclusively military terms. It is produced through many different discourses, inlcuding militaristic, televised reports, presidential speeches, historical documents, photo-journalism, the stories generated by *The Washington Post* and *The New York Times*, talk radio and television talk shows, movies, literature, advertising—each has a role to play in the definition of war. What readers can gain by dislocating the novel from its supposed literary category and relocating it as part of a wider set of social and economic discourses that are endlessly interrupting one another is this: one might read for new understandings of what have previously been understood as monolithic ethical paradigms—such as war—in discursive terms from a variety of sources. My study has drawn from a Foucauldian model of history as discourse in general, with specific attention to the forms unique to novelitic language in the late twentieth-century. A logical extension of this study then would be to juxtapose those other discourses more self consciously to see what readings present themselves, or, put slightly differently, to read those texts against one another. Such a move would necessarily gravitate away from the limits of literary criticism.

The importance of my study can be understood from three different angles. First, since most Americans living in this decade have not directly experienced war, but have, so to speak, indirectly experienced war through its simulation via television, film, or writing, it is important to ask what is it in our representations of war and in our modern understanding of the production of war that has led to the saturation of culture by war? For it is at this moment in history that war has so saturated the culture that one can no longer speak of a single "great" war, and violence seems to pervade every sphere of human life. Many critics and social historians have argued that the twentieth-century in general can be understood as a culture organized fundamentally around the concept of war (Fussell, 227; Virilo, 2-5; DeLanda, 5; Jeffords, xi; Theweleit, 314; Hanley, 4). In America, narratives of war may be

Conclusion: The Writing of War   123

particularly powerful in shaping a memory of war because "we"—a construction which excludes, among others, indigenous Native American populations—have never been occupied, invaded or bombed at home—or so we choose to tell ourselves. How the dominant culture tells the story of war, how the dominant nation remembers and forgets war determines its imagination around war and its place in it or out of it. But these are never the *only* stories of war.

The story of the white soldier male and his experiences at the front used to be axiomatic for our understanding of war. Before 1960, with a few notable exceptions such as Virginia Woolf, that story dominated our representations of war. The novels of war written between 1914 and 1940 teach us how to value war as a necessary evil in the growth and defense of nations and how to grieve for the soldier male. Since 1960 novels of war have displayed many different faces; the authority of the white soldier male has given way to other voices, such as women and minorities. Similarly, the stability of the battlefield is under question as representations and simulations achieve a new status in culture whereby viewers are bombarded with representations of war. In addition, the stability of history and language are being questioned through a variety of emerging discourses as well.

Thus, when one looks at novels such as Larry Heinemann's *Paco's Story*, the inability of the narrator to tell his story reflects a discursive crisis that is different from, though connected to, the crisis of the event. To tell a true war story turns out to mean the total breakdown of language and subjectivity. The discursive crisis of the narrator opens up a place where victim and killer, soldier and sniper, rapist and raped, merge. If we think of those binary oppositions as war roles, we can see that one story is upheld by their separation from one another and another story emerges from their conflation.

In Leslie Marmon Silko's novel *Almanac of the Dead* as well as Doris Lessing's science fiction novel *Shikasta*, readers get the chance to see what the story of war would look like if it was cut into a thousand pieces, if the weight given to specific wars, dates and national wounds was fragmented and dispersed over a new version of history in which those wars were merely signs in a sequence that never ends. In these works the cross-use of discourses and the breakdown of narrative content, reconfigured as a continual series of texts, signs and images, flattens history and displaces prior metanarratives. Looking at war as a discursive crisis gives us new ways to struggle with the writing and the unwriting of war.

Secondly, whereas the dominant form for the war novel prior to 1960 tended to be memoir, even as it employed a variety of formal strategies such as irony, the authors in my study show how that form is fundamentally inadequate, since memory has been redefined as a construct with many of the same features that fiction displays.[1] Looking at a novel like Kathy Acker's *Empire of the Senseless* shows us how psychological discourses and constructions of gender already contain the terms by which we "make war." Similarly, Silko's novel prohibits any single memory a place in history at all. Narrative fragmentation at the level of the breakdown of the subject, the division of the main character into split figures and the division of the plot into random pieces each suggest that no coherent form exists that would hold a stable "memoir" together.

Thirdly, bringing the combat zone to the home front, or the psychic front, or the sexual, racial, or representational front de-prioritizes the battlefield as the landscape of war. By emphasizing these new territories of war, the authors in my study emphasize how war is a habit of mind, a structure of consciousness, a cultural predisposition, a discursive realm. In fact, former war stories are brought into these texts as dead—because no longer attached to their historical moments—forms in the formal strategies of citation and pastiche, as if to say locating wars historically kills or represses all the other stories that might emerge. In the case of Don DeLillo's novel *White Noise*, the phenomenon of Hitler and the Cold War legacy of nuclear apocalypse are each displaced onto the forms that order our ordinary lives, such as television images, radio slogans, computer print-outs. As the phenomenon of Hitler is dislocated from history and commodified as a product on the open market, the story of individual identities dissolving under the pressure of ordinary life emerges. This is not to say that Nazi Germany has no value or ought to be forgotten; it is simply that our obsession with a certain version of honoring that memory keeps us from telling any other story of war or surviving it. As we look at representation itself, discursive possibilities open up for how we might let go of a certain valorized story of war and its combatants, killers and victims, and focus instead on our understanding of basic human identity and relationships, as well as how our technologically advanced world allows for the continued advancement of war as well as the possibility for avoiding it.

In the past, the arena of war has been understood as quintessentially masculine. Since 1960, disturbances in race, gender, and class arrangements at the front have changed the arena of war. Vietnam, Central America, and the Gulf War are prime examples. These new social configurations are reflected at home, but that reflection is often distorted, because a collision of roles and representations has produced a crisis that has served to show us the instability of our concepts of war and race, gender, and class. For example, the Gulf War certainly troubled conventional notions of masculinity and femininity in that women fought, were wounded, and died participating in that war, disturbing the constructs of both masculinity and femininity in the process. At the same time, the media was busy building images of women in the military that collided with their activities in the war. As Miriam Cooke and Angela Woollacott argue in their postscript to *Gendering War Talk*, women as soldiers have always been, and continue to be, a crisis in representation:

> Which pinup will last as the dominant image of the American woman in the military: the masculinized police-woman with the erect gun, reported

as the favorite of the American male soldier in the Gulf, or Gary Trudeau's drawing of a semi-stripped, frightened woman soldier? (322)

I bring this example up because it points to a fundamental question in my study, and that is, who fits into contemporary stories of war, and how do we read them? Up against government reports, televised productions, and media-hype, novels provide us with an alternative angle from which to view such a question. The novels in this study produce several different narrative positions for exploration: the character who turns from bellicosity to a critique of the self in *Shikasta*, the character who dissolves into land and more than sixty five different voices in *Almanac of the Dead*, the daughter in revision who is battling for subjectivity in *Empire of the Senseless*, the father who breaks down as the head of a nuclear family in the face of a nuclear ghost in *White Noise*, the white soldier male whose story drifts like dream (or television?) images in and out of a war that won't hold still in *Paco's Story*. These are the stories ordinarily repressed by received and conventional versions of war. Deconstructing war to its discursive parts shows us how we might build our way out.

The established canon of war fiction of this century has served as our collective memory of war. The technological and nuclear ages have fundamentally changed that. Along with those old spokespeople for war, government heads, academics, politicians, and news reporters, new voices are being amplified, those of enemies, victims, women, children, reluctant soldiers, those who refuse to fight, the poor, the marginalized. All are part of the new discourse of war. The novel has always been uniquely suited to memorialize war, but it is the contemporary novel, with its fragmented forms, that is uniquely suited to let those disparate voices co-exist, interrupt each other, torture one another, and yet survive. It may be possible that the older, valorized war story is dissolving through signification. In other words, it may be possible to demilitarize our understanding of war, if we can learn to read beyond the soldier's story and the forms that have prioritized it.

NOTE

1. I am speaking of the discourses of psychoanalysis and semiotics in particular, and a certain understanding based on the work of Freud, Lacan, and later feminist critics that language is structured like the unconscious. Narrative language provides more opportunities for charting the subconscious structures of language in general. See Julia Kristeva's *Revolution in Poetic Language* and Kaja Silverman's *The Subject of Semiotics*.

Bibiliography

Acker, Kathy. *Empire of the Senseless*. New York: Grove, 1988.

_____. *Algeria*. London: Aloe Books, 1984.

Adorno, Theodor. "Culture Industry Reconsidered." *New German Critique* n6 (Fall 1975): 3–19.

Allen, Paula Gunn. "Special Problems in Teaching Leslie Marmon Silko's Ceremony." *The American Indian Quarterly* (Fall, 1990): 379–387.

_____. "The Pscyhological Landscape of *Ceremony*." *American Indian Quarterly* 5(Spring, 1979): 10.

Anisfield, Nancy. "After the Apocalypse: Narrative Movement in Larry Heinemann's *Paco's Story*." Eds. Gilman, Smith. *America Rediscovered: Critical Essays on Literature and Film of the Vietnam War*. New York: Garland, 1990.

Anzaldua, Gloria. *Borderlands/La Frontera: The New Mestiza*. San Francisco: Aunt Lute Books, 1987.

Armstrong, Nancy. "The Rise of Feminine Authority in the Novel." *Why the Novel Matters*. Eds. Mark Spilka and Caroline McCracken-Flesher. Bloomington: Indiana University Press, 1990.

Auerbach, Erich. *Mimesis: The Representation of Reality in Western Literature*. Trans. Willard Trask. Princeton: Princeton Univeristy Press, 1953.

Bakhtin, M. M. *The Dialogic Imagination*. Trans. Caryl Emerson and Michael Holquist. Austin: University of Texas Press, 1981.

Baudrillard, Jean. "The Precession of Simulacra." *Art and Text*, 11 (September, 1983): 3–47.

Barthes, Roland. *The Responsibility of Forms*. Trans. Richard Howard. Berkeley: University of California Press, 1985.

Benjamin, Walter. *Illuminations*. Ed. Hannah Arendt. New York: Shocken, 1960.

Booth, Wayne. *The Company We Keep: An Ethics of Fiction*. Berkeley: University of California Press, 1988.

Brians, Paul. "Nuclear Family/Nuclear War." *Papers on Language and Literature* 26(Winter, 1990): 134–42.

Cahoone, Lawrence. *From Modernism to Postmodernism*. Cambridge: Blackwell Press, Inc., 1996.

Campbell, David. *Writing Security: United States Foreign Policy and the Politics of Identity*. Minneapolis: University of Minnesota Press, 1992.

Cockcroft, Eva. "Abstract Expressionism: Weapon of the Cold War." *Artforum* 15(June, 1974): 39–41.

Conrad, Joseph. *Heart of Darkness*. New York: New American Library, 1910.

Cooke, Miriam & Woolacott, Angela, Eds. *Gendering War Talk*. New Jersey: Princeton University Press, 1993.

Cooper, Helen, Munich, Adrienne and Suier, Susan, eds. *Arms and the Woman*. Chapel Hill: University of North Carolina Press, 1989.

De Landa, Manuel. *War in the Age of Intelligent Machines*. Eds. Jonathan Crary, Sanford Kwinter and Bruce Mau. New York: Swerve Editions, 1991.

DeLillo, Don. *White Noise*. New York: Penguin, 1986.

_____. *Running Dog*. New York: Penguin, 1978.

Dix, Douglas Shields. "Kathy Acker's Don Quixote: Nomad Writing." *The Review of Contemporary Fiction* (Fall, 1989): 57–62.

Draine, Betsy. *Substance Under Pressure: Artistic Coherence and Evolving Form in the Novels of Doris Lessing*. Madison: The University of Wisconsin Press, 1983.

Eagleton, Terry. "Capitalism, Modernism and Postmodernism." *New Left Review* 152(July/August, 1985): 60–73.

Eliot, T.S. *Selected Prose*. Ed. John Hayward. London: Faber and Faber, 1953.

Ehrenreich, Barbara. *The Hearts of Men: American Dreams and the Flight From Commitment*. Garden City: Anchor Press/Doubleday, 1983.

Elshtain, Jean Bethke & Tobias, Shiela, eds. *Women, Militarism and War*. Maryland: Rowman and Littlefield, 1990.

Elshtain, Jean Bethke. *Women and War*. New York: Basic Books, 1987.

Fanon, Frantz. *A Dying Colonialism*. Trans. Haakon Chevalier. New York: Grove Press, 1965.

Fishburn, Katherine. *The Unexpected Universe of Doris Lessing*. Westport: Greenwood Press, 1988.

Foucault, Michel. *The Order of Things: An Archeology of the Human Sciences*. New York: Pantheon, 1970.

Friedman, Ellen G. "Utterly Other Discourse." *Modern Fiction Studies* 34(Autumn, 1988): 353–70.

Bibliography

Fussell, Paul. *The Great War and Modern Memory.* New York: Oxford University Press, 1975.

_____. *Wartime: Understanding and Behavior in the Second World War.* New York: Oxford University Press, 1989.

Gibson, William. *Warrior Dreams: Violence and Manhood in Post- Vietnam America.* New York: Farrar, Straus and Giroux, 1994.

Gilbert, Sandra and Gubar, Susan. *No Man's Land: Sexchanges.* New Haven: Yale University Press, 1989.

_____. *No Man's Land: Letters From the Front.* New Haven: Yale University Press, 1994.

Guyotat, Pierre. *Eden Eden Eden.* Trans. Graham Fox. London: Creation Books, 1995.

Hanley, Lynne. *Writing War: Fiction, Gender and Memory.* Amherst: University of Massachusetts Press, 1991.

Harlow, Barbara. *Resistance Literature.* New York: Methuen, 1987.

Haraway, Donna. "The Biopolitics of Postmodern Bodies: Determinations of Self in Immune System Discourse." *Differences: A Journal of Feminist Cultural Criticism* 1(1989): 14.

Hassan, Ihab. *The Postmodern Turn.* Ohio State University Press, 1987.

Heinemann, Larry. *Paco's Story.* New York: Farrar, Straus, Giroux, 1979.

Hussey, Mark, ed. *Virginia Woolf and War.* Syracuse: Syracuse University Press, 1992.

Hemingway, Ernest. *A Farewell to Arms.* New York: Scribners, 1929.

hooks, bell. "Feminism as a Persistent Critique of History." *The Fact of Blackness.* Seattle: Bay Press, 1996.

Homberger, Eric. "The American War Novel and the Defeated Liberal." *Forum For Modern Language Studies* 21(Jan, 1985): 32–44.

Hughes, Robert. *The Shock of the New.* New York: Knopf, 1991.

Huyssen, Andreas. *After the Great Divide: Modernism, Mass Culture, Postmodernism.* Indianapolis: Indiana University Press, 1986.

Jacobs, Naomi. "Kathy Acker and the Plagiarized Self." *The Review of Contemporary Fiction* (Fall, 1989): 50–55.

Jameson, Fredric. *Postmodernism, or, The Cultural Logic of Late Capitalilsm.* Durham: Duke University Press, 1991.

_____. "Progress Versus Utopia; or, can We Imagine the Future?" *Science Fiction Studies.* 9(July, 1983), 147–58.

_____. "Postmodernism and Consumer Society." *Modern Drama.* Ed. W. B. Worthen. New York: Harcourt Brace College Publishers, 1995.

Jeffords, Susan. *The Remasculinization of America.* Bloomington: Indiana University Press, 1995.

Kaplan, E. Ann, ed. *Postmodernism and Its Discontents.* New York: Verso, 1988.

Kaplan, Carey & Rose, & Ellen C. *Doris Lessing: The Alchemy of Survival.* Athens: Ohio University Press, 1988.

Kermode, Frank. *The Sense of an Ending: Studies in the Theory of Fiction.* New York: Oxford University Press, 1967.

Kristeva, Julia. *Powers of Horror.* Trans. Leon Roudiez. New York: Columbia University Press, 1982.

_____. *Nations Without Nationalism.* Trans. Leon Roudiez. New York: Columbia University Press, 1993.

Jhally, Sut & Angus, Ian. *Cultural Politics in Contemporary America.* New York: Routledge, 1989.

Klein, Holer, ed. *The Second World War in Fiction.* London: Macmillian, 1984.

Lentricchia, Frank. *New Essays on Don Delillo.* Cambridge: Cambridge University Press, 1991.

Lessing, Doris. *Shikasta (Canopus in Argos Archives).* New York: Vintage, 1992.

_____. *A Small Personal Voice.* New York: Random House, 1975.

_____. *Prisons We Choose to Live Inside.* New York: Random House, 1987.

Lifton, Robert Jay. *Indefensible Weapons: The Political and Psychological Case Against Nuclearism.* New York: Basic, 1982.

Lyotard, Jean-Francois. *The Postmodern Condition: A Report on Knowledge.* Trans. Geoff Bennington and Brian Massumi. Minneapolis: University of Minnesota Press, 1989.

McHale, Brian. *Constructing Postmodernism.* New York: Routledge, 1992.

Mercer, Kobena. "Decolonization and Disappointment: Reading Fanon's Sexual Politics." *The Fact of Blackness.* Seattle: Bay Press, 1996.

Meyer, Eric. "Ford's War and (Post)Modern Memory." *Criticism* 32 (Winter, 1990): 81-99.

Misra, Kalidas. "The Amerian War Novel from World War II to Vietnam." *Indian Journal of American Studies* 14(July, 1984): 73–80.

O'brien, Tim. *The Things They Carried.* Boston: Houghton Mifflin, 1990.

Owens, Craig. *Beyond Recognition: Representation, Power and Culture.* Eds. Cott Bryson, Barbara Kruger, Lynne Tillman and Jane Weinstock. Berkeley: University of California Press, 1992.

Paris, Michael. *The Novels of World War II.* London: The Library Association, 1990.

Pérez, Castillo, Susan. "Postmodernism, Native American Literature and the Real: The Silko-Erdrich Controversy." *The Massachusetts Review* (Spring, 1981): 285–294.

Perrakis, Phyllis Sternberg. "The Marriage of Inner and Outer Space in Doris Lessing's *Shikasta*" in *Science Fiction Studies* 2(1990).

Peters, Nancy, ed. *War After War.* San Francisco: City Lights, 1992.

Bibliography

Peters, Cynthia, ed. *Collateral Damage: The "New World Order" at Home and Abroad*. Boston: South End Press, 1992.

Pick, Daniel. *War Machine: The Rationalization of Slaughter in the Modern Age*. New Haven: Yale University Press, 1993.

Pynchon, Thomas. *Gravity's Rainbow*. New York: Bantam, 1973.

Read, Alan. Ed. *The Fact of Blackness*. Seattle: Bay Press, 1996.

Scarry, Elaine. *The Body in Pain: The Making and Unmaking of the World*. New York: Oxford University Press, 1985.

Schwenger, Peter. "Writing the Unthinkable." *Critical Inquiry* 13 (Autumn, 1986): 33-48.

_____. "Circling Ground Zero." *Critical Inquiry* 13(Autumn, 1987): 252-61.

Schweninger, Laura. "Writing Nature: Silko & NAtive Americans as Nature Writers. *Melus* (Summer, 1993): 47-60.

Siegle, Robert. *Suburban Ambush: Downtown Writing and the Fiction of Insurgency*. Baltimore: John Hopkins University Press, 1989.

Silko, Leslie. *Almanac of the Dead*. New York: Penguin, 1991.

_____. *Ceremony*. New York: Signet Books of the New American Library, 1977.

_____. "Landscape, History, and the Pueblo Imagination." *On Nature: Nature, Landscape, and Natural History*. Ed. David Halpern. Berkeley: North Point Press, 1987.

Sontag, Susan. *Against Interpretation*. New York: Farrar Straus and Giroux, 1966.

Spilka, Mark and McCracken-Flesher, Caroline, eds. *Why the Novel Matters: A Postmodern Purplex*. Bloomington: Indiana University Press, 1990.

Swann, Edith. "Laguna Symbolic Geography and Silko's *Ceremony*." *American Indian Quarterly* 12(1988): 234-247.

Theweleit, Klaus. *Male Fantasies*. Vol. 1, *Women Floods Bodies History*. Minneapolis: University of Minnesota Press, 1987.

_____. *Male Fantasies*. Vol. 2, *Male Bodies: Psychoanalyzing the White Terror*. Minneapolis: University of Minnesota Press, 1989.

Thomson, Leslie and Cozart, William. "The Technology of Atrocity." *Ball State University Forum* 25(Autumn, 1984): 63-70.

Unger, Sheldon. *The Rise and Fall of Nuclearism*. Pennsylvania: Pennsylvania State University Press, 1992.

Virilio, Paul and Lotringer, Sylvere. *Pure War*. Trans. Mark Polizzotti. New York: Semiotext(e), 1983.

Vizenor, Gerald. *Narrative Chance: Postmodern Discourse on Native American Indian Literature*. Albuquerque: University of New Mexico Press, 1989.

Walsh, Edward. *Vietnam Images: War and Representation*. New York: St. Martin's Press, 1989.

Warrick, Patricia. *The Cybernetic Imagination in Science Fiction*. Cambridge: MIT Press, 1980.

Wilcox, Leonard. "Baudrillard, DeLillo's *White Noise*, and the End of Heroic Narrative." *Contemporary Literature* 32(1991).

Woolf, Virginia. *Between the Acts*. New York: Harcourt Brace, 1970.

_____. *Three Guineas*. New York: Harcourt Brace, 1963.

_____. *To The Lighthouse*. New York: Harcourt Brace, 1990.

_____. *The Voyage Out*. New York: Harcourt Brace, 1988.

Wallis, Brian, ed. *Art After Modernism*. New York: The New Museum of Contemporary Art, 1984.

Index

Acker, Kathy, 4, 9, 75, 99, 100, 103;
   Empire of the Senseless, 4, 9, 48, 52, 75, 75–94, 97, 123, 125;
   Don Quixote, 76, 77;
   The Childlike Life of the Black Tarantula, 76;
   The Adult Life of Henri Toulouse Lautrec, 76;
   Algeria, 77
Algerian Revolution, 77, 86, 87
allegory, 104, 105, 107, 110
Anzaldúa, Gloria, 117, 118;
   Borderlands, 117
Apocalypse Now, vii
Artaud, Antonin, 77
Atwood, Margaret: *The Handmaid's Tale*, 37
Auerbach, Erich: *Mimesis*, 7, 14

Bakhtin, M. M.: *The Diologic Imagination*, 36
Barthes, Roland, 3, 87, 88, 94, 99, 106, 107
Bataille, Georges, 77
battlefields, redefined, 126
Baudrillard, Jean, 3, 62, 64, 71; "simulacra," 66, 67, 70, 71
Benjamin, Walter, 104, 105–107, 110, 118
bodies of war:
   dissolving male body, 12, 28;
   wounded male body, 25–26, 28, 31;
   symbolic male body, 26–27;
   raped body, 26–27, 28–30, 31;
   mutating daughter's body, 87, 88;
   land as body, 108, 109
borders of war, 113–115, 117, 118
Bogart, Humphrey, 17
Booth, Wayne: *The Rhetoric of Fiction*, 6
Born on the Fourth of July, viii, 17
Burroughs, William, 82

capitalism, 61, 62, 76, 98, 100
Central America, 100, 124
children as soldiers, 47
Chomsky, Noam, vii
clan stories, 98
Close Quarters, viii
Colbey, Evelyn, 6

Cold War, The, 121, 124
colonization, 75–77, 78, 79, 83, 84,
    86–88, 91–93, 107
Coming Home, 17
consumerism, 61
Cook, Miriam: Gendering War Talk,
    126
Cooper, Gary, 17
Cruise, Tom, 17

death as narrative paradigm, 55, 58,
    69, 70–73
decolonization, 75, 77, 84, 86–88
deconstruction, 3
Deerhunter, The, vii
DeLillo, Don, 4, 9, 55, 99, 100, 103;
    White Noise, 4, 9, 55–73, 80,
    124, 125;
    Running Dog, 55;
    Endzone, 55;
    Americana, 55
Derrida, Jacques, 3, 55
Desert Storm, vii, 4
dialogism, 35, 36, 40, 45, 47
Diary of Anne Frank, The, vii
discourse, 8;
    cross-use of, 8;
    narrative discourse, 35, 36
dispossession, 108, 110, 111
drug wars, 100, 114
dystopian, 37
Dr. Strangelove, vii

Eco, Umberto: The Name of the Rose,
    56
Eliot, T. S., 11
Elshtain, Jean Bethke: Women and
    War, 38
Erdrich, Louise, 101

Fanon, Franz, 75, 77, 82, 93;
    A Dying Colonialism, 75, 83,
    84, 87;
    Black Skin, White Masks, 83,
    92;
    The Wretched of the Earth, 83,
    84, 92
Faulkner, William, 7
films of war, vii
Ford, Ford Maddox: Parade's End,
    viii, 6
Foucault, Michel, 3
Freud, Sigmund, 3, 62, 79, 82, 87,
    89–90, 101, n. 125
Frye, Northrup: Anatomy of Criticism,
    6
Full Metal Jacket, viii
Fussell, Paul, 5, 42;
    The Great War and Modern
    Memory, 5, 13, 14, 37, 121

Gee, Maggie: The Burning Book, 56
Gibson, James William, viii;
    Warrior Dreams, 17, 38
Gilbert, Sandra and Gubar, Susan, 37,
    53, 93;
    No Man's Land, 43
Graves, Robert, 13;
    Goodbye to All That, 15, 37, 43
Gunn Allen, Paula, 98, 102
Guyotat, Pierre, 77, 82, 91, 93;
    Eden, Eden, Eden, 87, 88,
    89–90, 93
Green Berets, The, viii, 17
Gulf War, vii, 4, 124

Hanley, Lynn: Writing War, 42, 50
Harlow, Barbara: Resistance

Literature, 99, 110
H.D., 16, 37, 53
Heinemann, Larry, vii, 4, 8, 11, 8, 103;
   Paco's Story, 4, 8–33, 123, 125
Hemmingway, Ernest, 7, 17, 18, 79;
   A Farewell to Arms, viii, 13, 14, 15, 18, 19, 37, 42, 43
Herr, Michael, vii, 11;
   Dispatches, viii
history
   as discourse, 3;
   as ruin, 103–106;
   as character, 111
Hitler, vii, 55, 59, 60, 63, 68, 121, 124
Hiroshima, 4
Hoban, Russell: *Ridley Walker*, 56
Holocaust, vii; Holocaust Studies, vii
hooks, bell, 92
Hughes, Robert, 3–4, 121; *Shock of the New*, 3–4
Huyssen, Andreas: *After the Great Divide*, 82, 121
Huxley, Aldous, 5

Jacobs, Naomi, 76, 78
Jameson, Fredric, 3, 7, 78, 79;
   Postmodernism, or, the Cultural Logic of Late Capitalism, 7, 62
Jeffords, Susan, 12;
   The Remasculinization of America, 12, 29–30
Joyce, James, 7, 79;
   Portrait of the Artist as a Young Man, 61

Kennedy (JFK), vii
Killing Fields, The, viii
Kristeva, Julia: *Revolution in Poetic*

Language, n.125

Lacan, Jacques, 3, 125
land as character, 108–110
Law of the Father, 85
LeGuin, Ursula: *Always Coming Home*, 37
Lessing, Doris, 4, 8;
   Shikasta, 4, 8, 38–53, 125, 125;
   A Small Personal Voice, 35;
   Children of Violence, 35;
   Prisons We Choose to Live Inside, 36
Lotringer, Sylver: *Pure War*, 9

Mailer, Norman: *The Naked and the Dead*, 6
male soldier, as paradigmatic war story, vii, viii, ix
Marx, Karl, 102;
marxism, 3, 102, 107
mestiza, 118
McHale, Brian, 57, 101;
   Constructing Postmodernism, 57, 68, 69
militant daughter, 85, 89–90
modernism, 6, 61–63, 79, 80, 99, 123, 122
multinationalism, 48

Native American, 97–102, 104, 105, 107, 108, 110, 113, 116, 119
Nazi Germany, 5, 55, 60
narrative form and war:
   narrative accumulation, 12, 20, 21;
   narrative appropriation, 8–10, 77, 79, 82, 84–86, 89–90, 92;
   narrative binaries, 51, 52;

narrative displace-ment, 55, 58, 68, 69, 72, 73, 124;
narrative fragmentation, 8–10, 97, 100, 101, 103, 106, 111, 112, 123, 124;
narrative pastiche, 8–10, 78, 79, 84–86, 89–90, 92;
narrative reflexivity, 8, 12, 18, 21, 24, 26, 27, 31
novel, the
   realist, 6, 15, 103;
   modernist, 6, 15, 103;
   history of 6, 13, 99, 122;
   novels of war, vii, 4, 5
nuclear apocalypse, 57, 126
nuclear family, 58, 67, 68
nuclear ideology, 9, 55, 56, 68
nuclear war, 55, 58, 73

O'brien, Tim: *Things They Carried, The*, viii, 11
Oedipal plot trajectory, 66, 73, 79, 85, 89–93, 94;
   family romance, 79
Owen, Wilfred, 43
Owens, Craig: *Beyond Recognition*, 67
oral tradition, 98, 102, 104, 106

patriarchy, 76, 79, 81, 83, 85, 88, 91, 93, 114
Patton, viii
Picasso, Pablo, 4, 5, 78;
   Guernica, 5
pirating, 79
plagiarism, 79
Platoon, 17
Plowman, Max: *Subaltern on the Somme*, 5
poststructuralism, 3, 53
postmodernism, 3, 7, 9, 53, 55, 57, 60–63, 67, 68, 71, 73, 76, 78, 79, 80, 86, 93, 94, 97, 99, 101–103, 107, 108, 110–112, 116, 119, 122
protagonist/antagonist dichotomy, 50
psychoanalytic discourse, 3, 53, 125
Pueblo tradition, 98
Pynchon, Thomas; viii;
   Gravity's Rainbow, viii, 57, 80

race wars, 100
rape, 12, 26–27, 28–30, 89–90
realism, 6
Red Badge of Courage, The, viii
Remarque, Erich Maria, 5;
   All Quiet on the Western Front, vii, 5, 13, 37
representation, vii, 13;
   films of war, vii, 17;
resistance, 97, 99, 100;
   narrative resistance, 105, 106, 110, 118, 119

sacred, 97, 98
de Sade, Marquis de, 77, 82
Sassoon, Siegfried, 5, 43;
   Memoirs of a Foxhunting Man, 5, 13
Saving Private Ryan, vii
Scarry, Elaine, 25;
   The Body in Pain, 25, 49, 53–54
Schindler's List, viii
Schwartzkopf, Norman, vii
sexual transgression, 93
Shields, Douglas Dix, 76
Siegle, Robert, 76, 93;
   Suburban Ambush, 76, 80
Silko, Leslie Marmon, 4, 9;
   Almanac of the Dead, 9, 48, 52, 97–119, 123, 125;
   Ceremony, 111

Silverman, Kaja: *The Subject of Semiotics*, n. 125
Slaughterhouse Five, vii
Sontag, Susan, 21
Stein, Gertrude, 79
storytelling, 106, 107, 108, 119
syntactic doubling, 12, 22, 23

technology, 68
television, 65, 66, 68, 69, 70, 121
terrorists, redefined, 47, 49, 88, 116
Thewveleit, Klaus: *Male Fantasies*, 38
Thin Red Line, The, viii
Three Kings, viii
Tolstoy, Leo, 6;
    War and Peace, 6

utopian, 37

Vietnam, vii, 7, 13, 16, 100, 121, 124;
    as crisis in representation, 16;
    as televised, 17, 23, 33
victim/victimizer dichotomy, 29, 31
violence as meaning, 18;
    spiritual and geographic violence, 103, 107, 109
Voight, John, 17

War,
    as representation vii-ix, 4;
    and art history, 2, 4;
    as crisis in representation 23, 57, 123;
    as family and cultural legacy, 35, 84;
    as history, 35;
    and literary form, 5, 43, 124;
    and memory, 14, 42, 46, 53, 123;
    and morality, 11;
    and photography, 21;
    and sexuality, 4, 29–30, 37, 53, 75–77, 79–94, 113–14, 123, 124;
    as story, 11–12;
    and technology, 4;
    as narrative discourse, ix, 40, 41, 43, 45, 46, 53, 122, 124;
    as structure of consciousness, 36, 39, 45–46, 48, 53;
    the "New War," ix;
    reading war, ix, 4;
    and science fiction, 39;
    and voyeurism, 28–30, 31, 32;
    and economy, 97, 98, 100, 104, 105, 109, 110, 112, 113, 115, 119
Waugh, Evelyn, 5
Wayne, John, 17
Wells, H. G., 38
woman as arsenal, 83, 84, 85, 87
women and war, 38, 43, 83
Woolf, Virginia, 7, 37, 38, 39, 45, 78, 79;
    To The Lighthouse, 16, 43, 61, 81, 82;
    Jacob's Room, 39, 53, 43;
    Between the Acts, 39, 82;
    Three Guineas, 39, 53, 80, 82;
    Mrs. Dalloway, 53;
    The Voyage Out, 81
World War I, vii, 6, 13, 14, 35, 100
World War II, vii, 6, 13, 35, 57, 100

Zapruder, vii